T0278097

Balance of Power

Balance of Power

CENTRAL BANKS AND THE FATE OF DEMOCRACIES

Éric Monnet

Translated from the French by
Steven Rendall

THE UNIVERSITY OF CHICAGO PRESS

Chicago and London

The University of Chicago Press, Chicago 60637

The University of Chicago Press, Ltd., London

© 2024 by The University of Chicago

Published 2024

Printed in the United States of America

33 32 31 30 29 28 27 26 25 24   1 2 3 4 5

ISBN-13: 978-0-226-83413-9 (cloth)

ISBN-13: 978-0-226-82547-2 (e-book)

DOI: https://doi.org/10.7208/chicago/9780226825472.001.0001

Originally published as *La Banque-providence: Démocratiser la banque
centrale et les monnaies* by Éric Monnet, © Éditions du Seuil et La Ré-
publique des Idées, 2021 and 2022 for the additions and updates.

Library of Congress Cataloging-in-Publication Data

Names: Monnet, Eric, 1983– author. | Rendall, Steven, translator.
Title: Balance of power : central banks and the fate of democracies /
    Éric Monnet ; translated from the French by Steven Rendall.
Other titles: Banque-providence. English (Rendall)
Description: Chicago : The University of Chicago Press, 2024. |
    Includes bibliographical references and index.
Identifiers: LCCN 2023036228 | ISBN 9780226834139 (cloth) |
    ISBN 9780226825472 (ebook)
Subjects: LCSH: Banks and banking, Central—Political aspects. |
    Welfare state. | Monetary policy.
Classification: LCC HG1854 .M66613 2024 |
    DDC 332.1/1—dc23/eng/20230830
LC record available at https://lccn.loc.gov/2023036228

♾ This paper meets the requirements of
ANSI/NISO Z39.48-1992 (Permanence of Paper).

This book was published in French in November 2021.
It was revised and expanded for the English edition
in the summer of 2022.

Contents

Central Banks
as Protectors

Central banks are contradictions. They are agencies of states, but they are not domains of governments. They provide credit to financial institutions to advance the public good, but they have no role in determining what the public good actually looks like. They adjust interest rates to promote (or sometimes counter) economic trends and social objectives, including employment and inflation rates, and to ensure that their credit environments remain viable. And increasingly, a central bank is a kind of social insurance for private and public credit—a lender of last resort when things turn sour in a financial system. In this role, we seem to learn more about them with each passing year and each passing crisis.

The challenge for central banks is to achieve their objectives of stabilizing the economy and providing for the public good without appearing outwardly political—favoring special interests or creating an economic environment that runs counter to the public will. In a time of increasing political polarization, the political stakes of central banks have become that much greater: by wielding their potentially unconstrained power to create credit and money, and often doing so in moments of crisis, they are increasingly accused of playing politics. The shortcomings of political systems make every action of a central bank resonate as a political stance for or against someone.

Indeed, the role of central banks stirs all manner of fantasies and legitimate misunderstandings. How can they simply create money from nowhere, whether to lend to banks or to buy up public debt? Is this kind of money creation even legitimate? If so, is a central bank really necessary at all? Commercial banks also create money when they grant loans, and private cryptocurrencies seemingly do the same thing. What gives central banks all this power, and do they know what they're doing with it?

The ostensibly unlimited power of the central banks since the 2008 financial crisis has raised all the more questions. Their purchase of public debt to finance government measures supporting the economy during the COVID-19 pandemic sowed the seeds of doubt, as the image of conservative, little-known institutions was at odds with their demonstrated power to finance virtually anything they want. The return of high inflation in rich countries fueled further confusion about the role of central banks. While these institutions were, according to late twentieth-century doctrine, devoted solely to the control of inflation, they appeared mostly helpless in the face of rising prices after COVID. In most countries, in fact, it was governments, not central banks, that were the first to react in the face of increased inflation, taking steps to minimize its impact on the workers who were most affected. However clumsily the process has emerged, central banks and other policy domains now share roles but without any declared institutional framework or economic doctrine.

This book argues that central banks' monetary policies and the bank's creation of money must be subjected to democratic control. These powers are too important to be managed solely by independent authorities operating as inward-facing technocrats.

Protecting people and states against the ups and downs of financial markets while maintaining the value of the currency (i.e., stable inflation) has long been the central banks' raison d'être. Over time, these banks have also assumed a role that is indirect but indispensable in the maintenance, legitimacy, and financing of the welfare state—the policy apparatus established after World War II to protect people from sources of hazard (especially employment and health hazards) and to promote greater financial equity over time. The hallowed stature of central banks within the economy is thus justified, but their excessive power—a symptom of dysfunctions in our political systems as well as in our financial systems—is not. As traditional sources of governance and policy grow less effective, the expansion of central banks' powers provides dangerous, incremental cover for reforms with no real oversight. Central bank interventions often serve as protection for states that are incapable of undertaking reforms of the financial system or of constructing a coherent credit policy or budgetary policy. It is therefore critical to understand and question the role of central banks today, while at the same time not treating them as isolated or idealized entities.

REDUCING UNCERTAINTY

Central banks' role as de facto insurance providers to financial markets and states, in principle for the benefit of the population, gives them a special place in the state apparatus and the economy. However, this should not give them undue leeway without checks and balances. As an institution serving the public good, the central bank must be subject to democratic debate and institutional balance of power—not as a purely technical manager dealing with matters isolated from the rest of economic and social policy.

The point is not to question the independence of central banks—that is, the principles according to which they make their decisions without instructions from the government. Indeed, such independent administrative authorities are a legitimate component of modern democracies, and they are part of the balance of powers.[1] Democracies are a system of checks and balances, not the unlimited power of the parliamentary majority. Moreover, the autonomy of the central bank can be seen as essential for its ability to come to the aid of the state, if need be, when the government fails to do so. The history of central banks shows that such independence has always been one of their defining characteristics, albeit to differing degrees. Central banks' very existence is justified by the fact that people believe that money is more efficiently managed by an institution that is separate from a Treasury department or ministry of finance.

Even so, the values that justify this independence (imperatives such as reflexivity, accountability, impartiality, and transparency) require strengthening if they are to be adapted to the central banks' current activities. Independence does not mean that there is no consultation or coordination with other policies or democratic structures; that is what has been too long forgotten.[2]

It is possible, in other words, to accept the protective role of the central bank while also updating the terms of its independence. In fact, it is all the more necessary because—like other public administrations since the turn toward neoliberalism in the 1980s—the policy of the central banks has sometimes deviated in recent decades from the principles of the welfare state (i.e., maximizing the welfare of the public) that once characterized it. This has produced disastrous consequences for the economy, including financial instability and the proliferation of inequalities. The last decades have seen many central bankers more preoccupied with giving lectures on the liberalization of the labor market or the privatization of retirement plans than with sticking to the objectives of financial stability or targeting inflation.

The central banks, as we see them today (that is, as public institutions that are not subordinated to the goal of increasing private shareholders' profits), were largely created after World War II. Central banks have a long history, but they were profoundly reformed in the middle of the twentieth century, at the same time as the policies that made up the welfare state and with similar objectives. (The United States is to a certain extent an exception in this regard, to which I shall return.) They are no longer controlled by private shareholders, and their money creation is no longer limited by gold reserve laws. They were quickly integrated into the state apparatus and into a set of macroeconomic policies that had not existed earlier in their history. Starting in the 1980s, the strengthening of central bank independence relative to governments reduced the range of the central banks' activities. This has not, however, led to a questioning of the fact that they should be under parliamentary oversight, independent of private interest, and in charge of macroeconomic policy on behalf of the common good. There has been no return to the principles of central banking that prevailed before World War II. Yet the definition of central bank independence formulated at the end of the twentieth century was not well equipped to address the new economic and democratic challenges of the early twenty-first century. We are left with an unsustainable gap between what central banks actually do and the institutional framework that defines their responsibility.

The macroeconomic principles on which central banks and the welfare state were conceived were the same: countercyclical policies intended to protect individuals from economic risk (including price and financial instability) and reduce overall uncertainty. But these historical and conceptual links between central banks and the welfare state are rarely made explicit. Drawing attention to them does not mean to suggest that we should ask the central bank to pay for welfare benefits. The point is to recognize that, like other pillars of the welfare state in capitalist societies, the central bank performs a *function of managing risks and reducing uncertainty.* Just as the risks evolve, so too must the institutions. As the twentieth-century economic anthropologist Karl Polanyi said, the central bank's policy is always a form of interventionism that evolves over time in accord with the nature of the state. It reflects the choices made regarding distribution and power in society.

This necessity of institutional evolution is why many central banks (including the European Central Bank, contrary to what is often claimed) have in their mandate not only an objective of price stability but also the objectives of full employment, social welfare, or even environmental protection. These objectives involve protecting the economy against the failures of banks and financial markets and, in some cases, providing an alternative to them. The result is a long-term management and insurance function over any given time horizon, one that includes the objective of a stable currency (represented by the inflation rate or the exchange rate depending on the country) but, most of the time, is not limited to it.

The insurance function may be less obvious, but it is all the more important today for the management of public debt and the ecological transition. It is based on a dynamic view of the insurance function of the welfare state: investing and regulating today in order to avoid paying compensation tomorrow. The importance of long-term thinking for monetary policy (*time-consistency*) has often been considered by economists in the context of price stability, but this traditional objective cannot be separated in practice from other social and economic objectives. Central banks need to be concerned about anything that might affect what they are responsible for: the value of money.

Finally, examining the political and economic identities of the central bank also implies carefully defining its scope of actions.

We must guard against the undemocratic temptation to entrust control of the whole political economy to the power of creating money. Monetary policy must reduce uncertainty and support other economic and social policies with an eye toward coordinating them—not substituting itself for them. The first part of this book emphasizes these distinctions, which are important for democratic equilibrium, and the necessity of not equating the central bank with a public investment bank or the ministry of finance.

NEW ROLES AND THE DEMOCRATIC LEGITIMACY OF CENTRAL BANKS

Central banks are traditionally in charge of ensuring macroeconomic stability (avoiding excessively high levels of inflation and unemployment) and financial stability (avoiding crises), issuing bank notes, and monitoring payments. This book shows that in the years to come, central banks will play a key role, directly or indirectly, in three new domains: the ecological transition, the price of public debt, and putting into circulation a new form of digital money to counteract private initiatives (cryptocurrencies).

The actions of central banks will therefore necessarily encroach on other domains of political and social economy, and their legal independence does not give them sufficient legitimacy to act alone in their new domains. How, then, can the central banks' democratic legitimacy be reconstructed and their policies made more effective for the common good? To answer this question, we need to move away both from a vision of democracy confined solely to elections and from a vision of independent authorities reduced solely to the principle of delegated power. These two views are generally articulated and defended together. To put it schematically, they justify the central bank's legitimacy by virtue of the institution's ability to act in accord with a mandate provided by a delegation of people.

The role of the parliament or congress is then only to make sure that the central bank properly respects this mandate. In this perspective, the decision-making process and the conditions under which this process participates in a redefinition of the mandate over time are not put in question.

Paradoxically, this perspective is shared both by those who believe that the independence of the central bank is heresy and by those who defend it at any cost. The technocratic defense of central bank independence does away with the evolution of the mandate's interpretation, and especially with the question of how to structure the democratic legitimacy of that evolution, which is irreducible to the legal framework. Today, it produces calls for a return to the past that offers little basis for guiding monetary policy as it is actually practiced by central banks. Central bank laws are essential to provide a democratic basis for these institutions, but the mandate is neither well defined nor narrow. The contract between the central bank and the people is fundamentally incomplete because—as the last fifteen years have reminded us—it cannot foresee every contingency. A technocratic approach to central banking therefore neglects this fundamental question: Who has the right to make decisions on the "missing things" in this contract, and how? On the other hand, calls to put an end to the independence of the central bank and to make monetary policy entirely subordinate to budgetary policy view the central bank's legitimacy solely as a result of elections and leave no room for the unelected bodies that are nonetheless part of our democratic life. They refuse to recognize the need for an institutional balance of power between the budgetary and monetary realms and overlook the fact that a central bank is a bank, not a printing press.

These two opposite views give little thought to the construction of a democratic legitimacy beyond a validation after the fact by the people's representatives. And more concretely, these concepts

8

fail to articulate how we as citizens can judge whether a central bank has made sound decisions with respect to curbing inflation, ensuring financial stability, or encouraging the energy transition, or how these decisions complement (or fail to complement) other governmental policies. The democratic legitimacy of an institution cannot be reduced to monitoring after the fact by elected representatives or to the transparency of decision-making processes. The foundation of democratic legitimacy is an institution's ability to demonstrate that these choices were made impartially, taking into account all the possible options, and with a full knowledge of their social, political, and economic consequences.

This requires, then, recognizing that there are other options—other means toward democracy—and giving them full consideration. The role of parliament is essential for overseeing the central bank, but democracy must also see itself as a set of nonelectoral procedures and functionalities that ensure that decisions are transparent, proportionate to the objectives, and based on the presentation of opposing and balanced arguments.

LIMITING THE POWER OF CENTRAL BANKS

The view of the democratic legitimacy of central banks that I am proposing here does not seek to expand their powers infinitely—or even their objectives as defined by their legal status—or to involve them in all aspects of the economy. On the contrary, this book exists because I believe that there is a real danger to democracy in expecting too much from unelected institutions with an ill-defined balance of power. I consider the immense power given to central banks in recent decades, with little oversight and explicit coordination with the rest of economic policy, to be a symptom of a democratic crisis. Paradoxically, it is because central banks became too independent that governments unloaded their problems on them. The unchecked rise of central banks often represents a failure by governments to take care of their responsibilities.

Here I propose an improvement of the deliberative process that seeks to force central banks, governments, and society to explore other options—and in particular, whether institutions other than central banks might be capable of implementing policies to achieve similar goals. In this book's first chapter, I emphasize the historical and conceptual distinctions between the central bank, the Treasury, and public development banks. Clearly distinguishing among these three institutions is fundamental if we seek to coordinate their policies. Distinction and coordination are as necessary for the balance of powers as they are for economic efficiency. To avoid an omnipotent central bank, we have to connect the central bank's policy with all the public policies related to finance—what is generally called *credit policy*. Paradoxically, it is because these interactions were poorly conceived and articulated at the end of the twentieth century that central banks found themselves in an omniscient but ill-defined position after the 2008 financial crisis. The landscape after COVID showed us that this perspective also applies to inflation. Those for whom controlling inflation was assumed to be the task of the central bank have been surprised to see that central banks are no better placed than other institutions to anticipate or address price increases. The fact that the stability of prices is a goal of monetary policy does not mean that it should be barred from the consideration and intervention of budgetary, financial, price control, wage, and environmental policies, not to mention geopolitical stakes.

CREDIT POLICY

Credit policy refers to all types of state interventions that deal with the development and allocation of credit and money and their distributional consequences. It is distinct from *monetary policy*—that is, how central banks influence macroeconomic aggregates (money, prices, GDP, etc.), regardless of distributional effects. In addition to the conduct of monetary policy, central banks participate—whether they want to or not—in a country's credit policy because their actions influence the volume and distribution of credit in the economy. A central bank's influence in this context depends on how it chooses to make loans to certain financial intermediaries or to purchase certain types of financial securities. Increases in interest rates have different repercussions on credit too, depending on the sector and the type of borrower or financial asset. But credit policy is also much larger than the simple role of a central bank: states intervene in this area in many ways, from financial regulation to preferential granting of credit in certain sectors (including indirectly, through subsidies, taxes, and specialized institutions). The role of the central bank, then, has to reflect its status as one of several actors operating in a space that is constantly changing; the bank's role cannot be fixed and immutable because it depends on economic contingencies or the evolution of long-term state objectives. Central banks have been involved in credit policy in many ways, on a large scale since 2008, and even more during the COVID-19 crisis in the United States. Yet a coherent framework for central banks' credit policy is missing. As we shall see, the creation of macroprudential policy authorities in the 2010s was an attempt to provide such a framework, but their scope remains limited and concerns only financial stability.

During earlier periods of history, when states were more interventionist in the economic sphere than they are today, the central bank participated more explicitly and assertively in the credit policy defined by governments and other public institutions. But it was not the leader, and certainly not the alpha and omega of the policy space that it is today. Its historical role was mostly supportive, especially through its functions of providing insurance and reducing uncertainty. This legacy of restraint poses real questions about how today's more powerful central banks intervene in the looming crises of our time. It would be dangerous and unprecedented, for example, to do away with the role of taxes in the financing of the state and in reducing inequalities based on a belief that the central bank can easily finance any public debt. It would be just as counterproductive to leave the policy of environmental financing in the hands of the central bank without involving the private sector through new credit standards and changes in management practices, as well as the public financial sector through targeted long-term financing. Rethinking the role of the central bank alongside a general credit policy overseen by the state therefore requires doing a better job of delimiting and restraining the bank's functions. And this in turn requires thinking holistically about a state's credit policy.

From this perspective, we have much to learn from history. Any profound reform of central banks during earlier eras, including the banks' creation, has always been linked to restructuring of the banking and financial systems.[3] Although the central banks themselves obviously play a role in the organization of the financial system, their instruments and missions develop in relation to the private systems of money and credit that they partially regulate. Reforming the central bank requires reforming the financial system, if only to ensure that the two are not functioning on different planes; addressing the two together provides the basis on which to establish an effective and legitimate money and credit policy. Today we are obliged to rethink the organization of credit policy in societies based on our shared, changing economic landscape: the imperatives of long-term investing in the ecological transition; the growing role played by nonbank financial institutions; the proliferation of digital currencies. Consideration of these kinds of issues is a precondition for recasting the policy of central banks. Thus, it is essential to give these matters thought and especially to institutionalize them in order to create a point of connection within the state apparatus and democratic functioning where credit policy can be discussed. As in the past, the shape of the financial system and the objectives of credit policy will ultimately depend on each country's particular economic and political characteristics. While it is possible to find examples from the past that can stimulate reflection, it is also the case that democratic standards and aspirations in today's democracies are usually much higher—and rightly so—than they were centuries, even decades, ago.

PROPOSALS FOR REFORM

I offer a few proposals for reform that would bring the central bank's activities into harmony with these principles of democracy. I shall discuss them largely in the context of Europe (where I live and work), then mention a few preconditions that must be met by other democratic countries, including the United States.

The role of central banks and their democratic framework cannot follow a single model throughout the world; on the contrary, these institutions must adapt to the political particularities of each country as well as to very different financial systems. Critically, the reflections pursued in this work will have little applicability to nondemocratic countries such as China. But that is not to say that China is irrelevant to this discussion. The way in which coordination between the government, central banks, and public or private banks is established in China should be discussed in order to understand this alternative, nondemocratic model of central banking, which will necessarily have an influence on the world order.

Within the eurozone, my first and most critical proposal is to provide structural sources of economic expertise for the parliament that would allow it to communicate on equal terms with the central bank on matters of economics—not, as is typically the case, to leave it solely to central bankers to make decisions that shape the future of our financial system. An institution (it might be called the "European Credit Council") that would report to the European Parliament could be assigned to study the consequences of monetary and credit policies for the economy as a whole, and also to make proposals to the central bank (and other institutions involved in credit policy), so that its policy might fully complement other European economic, social, and credit policies. This would be a first step toward a new kind of coordination between monetary policy and other policies regarding the financing of the welfare state (fiscal policy) and of long-term investments (credit policy). The credit council would not make decisions, but its purpose would be twofold: to reinforce the balance of power between the parliament and the central bank, and to act as a forum for assessment and reflection on coordination between the various agencies or public administrations involved in credit policy.

Democratizing the central banks also involves recreating a special connection between the central banks and citizens. From a historical point of view, the role and financial influence of the central banks have witnessed unprecedented growth in recent years; by contrast, the direct services that they perform for individuals or small businesses (currency exchange, deposits, loans) have dwindled to almost nothing. The disconnect this has created is indefensible, giving rise to a situation in which citizens have no understanding of the function of central banks, which prevents any broad sense of ownership and obstructs democratic debate. Paradoxically, the dematerialization of currency—and the creation of digital currencies by central banks that it implies—may provide an opportunity to reestablish this bond by strengthening and making more visible the *public service performed by currency.*

Before examining how current monetary policy functions and the many elements at stake in its operation, and before reflecting on institutional reforms, let us begin by exploring what a central bank does and how it is connected with the welfare state, credit policy, and the banking and financial system.

Central Banks, Money, and the Welfare State

The absence of a reasoned, informed debate and an institutionalized space for discussing monetary questions is itself a problem. Indeed, monetary policy is a core feature of the collective dimension of a democratic society and of the very legitimacy of the state. Confidence in the state currency is a necessary condition not only for economic exchange between individuals but for the state's ability to collect taxes and issue debt as well. Monetary policy is based on this confidence; its goal is to maintain it.

THE MONETARY SYSTEM AS A PUBLIC GOOD

The monetary system is a public good: everyone benefits from its existence, and one person's use of it does not compromise its use by others. In contrast, it is obvious that money itself is *not* shared, and at any given moment a unit of money that belongs to a single individual belongs to no one else. But the value of that money—of the currency—is a collective good. A society will suffer if money is no longer worth anything, if it is no longer accepted as a means of payment, or if it is impossible to borrow temporarily in order to resolve cash-flow problems.

The role of the central bank, then, is to guarantee the stability of this monetary system against the two main risks it may engender: major inflation and financial crisis. Inflation reflects the loss of confidence in a currency as a means of exchange and as a reserve of value. If people in a society believed that their currency would soon be worthless, everyone would immediately seek to get rid of it—to cut their losses by exchanging it for other things—as soon as possible. Inflation puts a society on this path, or at least the first steps of it, through the loss of a currency's value: the purchasing power of a ten-dollar bill is less if consumer prices have increased. But a moderate price inflation, the kind seen in the aftermath of the COVID crisis, is usually not caused by a loss of confidence in the currency: it arises primarily when the demand for goods exceeds the supply, and it may be increased by the market power of the companies that determine prices. It is only when a certain threshold is crossed that people consciously wish to get rid of their currency because they anticipate its loss of value.

While this currency-shedding phenomenon has been observed during periods of hyperinflation (which is conventionally defined as a rise in prices of more than 50 percent per month), it can accompany lower rates of inflation, too. In these instances, people prefer to invest in nonmonetary assets such as real estate, or try to buy foreign currencies to protect themselves from rising prices. Meanwhile, the loss of confidence in a currency leads businesses to increase prices and employees to demand higher salaries in order to protect themselves against the currency's anticipated loss of value. In theory, therefore, we know relatively well what can lead to and accentuate a currency's loss of value. But in practice, it's all a question of the threshold—that is, the point where collective beliefs shift and behaviors follow. More often than not, such behaviors are not conducive to a thriving state or society.

In addition to inflation's tendency to raise uncertainty about the value of a currency, the other reason to limit inflation has to do with its political and social consequences—notably, the fact that the poorest suffer most from an increase in prices if salaries do not rise proportionately.[1] Somewhat paradoxically, this is especially true in societies in which the welfare state is strong—where redistributive policies exist, but the nature of the policies is that they are not adjusted for inflation (or with a lag). On the other hand, a society without inflation is often regarded as economically stagnant and may in turn also disadvantage the poor: in the face of a perceived slowdown, capital becomes a greater source of income, while income from (and for) labor is diminished.

The acceptable level of inflation is therefore not an inviolable economic law. Deciding at what point inflation excessively disrupts society by damaging the system of payments and putting parts of society at a disadvantage is thus a question that does not concern the central bank alone. In fact, in countries with a fixed exchange rate, the rate of exchange between local currencies and foreign currencies—another measure of the value of the currency—is determined by the government, not by the central bank.[2] Ultimately, it is the central bank that is entrusted with the task of avoiding a loss of confidence in the currency—but that always leaves ample room for interpreting the threshold at which monetary stability is called into question. This is all the more true when the exchange rate is flexible and thus the currency's value with regard to foreign currencies is not set by the government.

The central bank can intervene in the value of the currency by restricting bank credit (either by raising interest rates or by taking steps to ration credit directly), which causes the excess demand for consumer goods to decrease in relation to supply. It can also play a role in keeping individuals and businesses from losing confidence in the future value of the currency. This requires the central bank's commitment to use its credit-control instruments or asset purchases, if necessary, and to maintain a defined threshold beyond which the rate of inflation is considered too high (or, in some countries, through its commitment to maintain the fixed rate of exchange). But the central bank's policy is not the only thing that affects consumer prices. Fiscal policy and financial cycles can also influence consumption and thus potentially prices. Some countries and industries have prices that are regulated by the state. And most often it is businesses and employees that set prices and salaries, using negotiation mechanisms that may vary greatly from one country to another; this justifies the coordination of different macroeconomic policies within a country. The policy of price stability, like other economic policies, is inherently rife with dilemmas and trade-offs. Simple, consensual solutions do not exist. Here the question of democracy and the justification of central banks' objectives arises once again; we will return to it later.

Unlike inflation, financial crises involve a loss of confidence in credit, which in normal times is the counterpart to money.[3] A financial crisis occurs when it is expected that banks or other borrowers (businesses, households) will default and that no one will lend money to them. A financial crisis may also cause a loss of confidence in the currency, which leads to hyperinflation, especially when the financial crises take the form of abrupt cessations of the inflow of foreign capital, as in the case of the hyperinflation in Germany in 1921–1923, or more recently, in Lebanon. But in reality the opposite is more common: where there is a banking or financial crisis, savings accumulate in the sole form that will be considered sufficiently secure (paper or coin, public debt, foreign currency, depending on the case), and the system seizes up, resulting in a decrease in the creation of debt, then deflation. Deflation is characterized by a situation in which economic activity—and thus prices—decrease while unemployment increases. That is what happened during the Great Depression of the 1930s,[4] a crisis that left a mark on the history of central banks and profoundly changed their nature.

Thus, a central bank must guarantee confidence not only in the currency (the means of payment) but also in the credit system and its component parts—private banks. This does not mean that central banks are obligated to save all banks, no matter the circumstances. But it does mean that the central bank has to ensure that if any given institution declares bankruptcy, it does not take the rest of the financial system down with it.

The intricate interweaving of a system of credit and the management of a currency by a central bank emerged on a large scale during the nineteenth century.[5] Gradually, the equivalence was constructed between money issued by the central bank (in the form of banknotes or bank deposits; see chapter 2) and money issued by commercial banks (in the form of deposits by businesses or households). In other words, the system guaranteed that the money held by an individual in a bank account could automatically be converted into sovereign currency—into a bank bill issued by the central bank and certified by the state. This equivalence has now become so customary—at least in wealthy, economically stable countries—that we are no longer even aware that these are two different types of money. But the banking crises of the 1930s revealed that this system was in fact unfulfilled: central banks were not prepared to assume this equivalence when there was a systemic banking crisis. Many commercial banks around the world had to close, and this led to a disconnect between the system of credit borne by these banks (which collapsed) and the monetary system guaranteed by the central bank (which was protected in most countries).[6]

The consequence of this crisis was a reorganization of the banking system, and with it a new role for central banks. The new organization was founded on the idea that banks had to be strictly regulated to ensure the survival of the equivalence between the sovereign currency issued by the central bank and bank money (i.e., deposits held at commercial banks).[7] The objective of the regulation of banks was obviously to strengthen financial stability in an attempt to forestall further crises. But it was also, and above all, a question of creating counterparties for the banks to what was becoming a form of insuring—implicitly or explicitly depending on the country—their activities by the central bank.

We have not really emerged from this public-private partnership, which was forged in the 1930s and 1940s in most countries. The questions raised by these partnerships also persist. It remains an open question how best to determine the conditions on which the state delegates the public service of money creation to private banks. The financial liberalization during the 1980s and 1990s further changed the situation in two respects. It eased the regulatory conditions (whether with regard to the regulation of activities or to governance) to give commercial banks more freedom of choice while at the same time retaining the insurance provided by the central bank. It also enabled the development on a large scale of new, private financial actors ("shadow banks") that do not source money from deposits, like commercial banks do, but interact extensively with those commercial banks in the money market.[8]

The crisis of the 1930s revealed a poor fit at the time between the role of the central banks and the functioning of the banking system. The financial crisis of 2008–2009, for its part, revealed a poor fit between the changes in the financial system over the two preceding decades and the role of the central banks in managing the credit system. Financial stability is no longer solely a matter of the equivalence between the money issued by the central bank and the money issued by commercial banks; today's financial system is increasingly disconnected from bank deposits. Accordingly, the links between currency as a public good and financial stability must be rethought.

THE CENTRAL BANK AND GOVERNMENT DEBT

What applies to a bank can also be applied to the credit of the state, otherwise known as government debt. If—as is the case in most modern states—government debt is a financial asset that banks exchange and hold collectively, then when a state's credit fails, private credit will fail as well. Ensuring the stability of the state's financing is thus a condition for financial and monetary stability in the private sector too.

Unfortunately, questions about the links between government debt and central banks are often formulated in ways that are both binary and unrealistic: Must the central bank finance the state directly by creating money? Would that kind of financing amount to giving up the central bank's independence?

These formulations misconceive the problem, for at least two reasons. First, central bank independence has not always ruled out direct (controlled and limited) monetary financing of government debt.[9] Second, and most important, central banks execute their policies by buying and selling government debt on financial markets. It is not a matter of "direct" financing, because that function cannot be carried out solely at the government's request; a bank must have first bought the government bond that the central bank then buys. (Specifically, this means that the state must first issue its debt and sell it to banks "at market conditions." The central bank can later buy it back, but nothing obliges it to do so.) But—and this is the key point—to be able to conduct its monetary and financial policy, the central bank also needs the price of government debt to be stable.

Government debt is in fact indispensable for the functioning of financial markets because banks and other financial institutions not only invest in it but also use it as a guarantee (collateral) for borrowing more. For this, government debt must be equivalent to money; that is, it must be a very liquid asset that can be rapidly and securely exchanged. To guarantee the stability of the monetary and financial system, the central bank must therefore act in such a way that government debt and money are almost indistinguishable from one another. In our current economies, few citizens realize this because most people don't trade government debt on a day-to-day basis. But banks and other financial institutions do. And a primary function of the central banks is to be at the center of the banking and financial system to grease its wheels.

The purchase of government debt by the central banks is not new (see chapter 3, figure 4). On the contrary, it is one of the primary functions of many of the central banks, starting with the Bank of England in the seventeenth century. But today's situation is unique because of the importance that government debt has assumed since the 1990s: as a safe asset in the functioning of financial markets.[10] The contemporary role of government debt is a consequence of two fundamental changes from the financial liberalization period of the 1980s. First, the share of total public debt traded in the market increased in all countries, meaning that—for wealthy countries whose government debt was considered a safe asset—the majority of today's government debt is treated as a liquid asset that financial actors exchange.[11] In the financial system, government debt is effectively a form of money. This was not the case during the formative period after World War II, when much of government debt was constituted by actual direct loans to the government, and banks were required to hold government debt as part of their assets, including assets in the form of Treasury deposits. And unlike the situation in the nineteenth century, when government debt was also put on the market, today's government debt is no longer held directly by individuals. Second, trading in government debt has become the preferred form of interactions between the banking sector and financial institutions that are not banks—investment firms, hedge funds, insurance companies—which together account for a set of interactions over which the central bank has less direct control.[12] Through its ubiquity, government debt has become one of the pillars of global financial stability more broadly. This makes government debt a source of mutual dependence between governments, central banks, and financial markets. But the terms of this mutual dependence have in large measure escaped citizens' notice.

THE CENTRAL BANK AND THE WELFARE STATE

The central bank's role as guarantor of monetary and financial stability is of long standing. These principles have guided central banks throughout their history, but especially since the nineteenth century. Over time, the central banks have upheld these imperatives more or less willingly and successfully.[13] In moments of failure, economies have faced uncontrollable inflation (hyperinflations following wars or, to a lesser degree, the inflationary period of the 1970s) or deflationary banking crises, like those of the Great Depression in the 1930s. But increasingly, and especially after World War II, the role of central banks as money and finance's guarantor has become even more essential, for at least two reasons.

First, societies (and people) are increasingly banked and financialized. Wages today are usually deposited directly into bank accounts, part of a larger trend in which households' use of consumer banks for day-to-day living (including credit) has become a normal, even essential, phenomenon. This was not the case before the 1950s. Second, the nature of government debt has changed through the development of the welfare state. We can think of the term *welfare state* as describing the ways in which the state intervenes in the social and economic domains in order to provide a service to citizens and to protect them from hazards that could affect their income (unemployment, illness, retirement, financial crisis, etc.). In the same way that earlier governments went into debt in order to finance wars (and some still do, unfortunately), today's debt is produced in part to fund the welfare state, that is, the well-being of its citizens (education, health care, the judicial system, etc.). The social issues presently associated with government debt are thus entirely different from those preceding the second half of the twentieth century.

Therefore—without being always explicit or demanded—the central bank cannot be conceived independently of the welfare state. The critical role of government debt within today's financial system only cements the relationship between the two. Central banks further contribute to the welfare state, albeit indirectly, by protecting economies from excessive inflation, financial crises, and deflation, any of which would sap the foundations and the organization of the state. It is rightly argued that the central bank is the bank of banks. But people tend to minimize or qualify its other major role: guarantor of the legitimacy and financing of modern states. The direct or indirect support provided by central banks to governments, companies, and banks during the COVID-19 crisis shows this clearly.

Recognizing the role of the central bank within the welfare state is also not new. It is precisely on these grounds that European central banks were nationalized and integrated into public administrations after the Great Depression and World War II; prior to that, they had been no more than private bankers' clubs on which the state conferred the right to issue and manage the currency (although this privilege was constrained by the requirement of gold reserves).[14]

The integration of the central bank into the state apparatus was not limited to the purchase of capital by the government or a change in bank employees' professional status. And as we know from the banks' status today, it did not necessarily coincide with a loss of their structural independence. In Western Europe, the central banks' nationalization was mostly a matter of integrating the central bank into a coherent macroeconomic- and financial-policy whole that could keep the lid on inflation (for many countries, the main challenge of the postwar period and reconstruction) and encourage economic growth. This holistic macroeconomic perspective was new, the policy heir to the increase in economic intervention by governments in the 1930s and during the war. In addition, it resulted in the formulation of new macroeconomic and financial statistics. And it was also between the 1930s and the 1950s that every country created a central bank, making these institutions standard pillars of economic policy alongside fiscal policy.

In some countries, including France and Italy, this movement of states regaining control of the financial system was described as the "nationalization of credit," in which the central banks' new functions (along with the end of the primacy of the gold standard) were included.[15] The Board of Governors of the Federal Reserve System that governs the Federal Reserve System (the "Fed") in the United States was already a public administration during the interwar period. The New Deal reforms of 1933 and 1935 gave it increased weight, albeit at the expense of the twelve regional banks of the Federal Reserve System that are owned by private shareholders. The explicit goal of the Fed's new governor, Mariner Eccles, with President Franklin D. Roosevelt's support, was to make the central bank a genuine, centralized, federal administration and to limit the influence of private bankers on its decisions. The centralization of power and the increased integration of the public central bank within the state apparatus was also advanced by other means, including policies for financing private enterprises that were more proactive, in keeping with the New Deal's programs of economic reconstruction.[16] Whereas World War II had reduced the Fed's room to maneuver because of the sudden predominance of financing government debt, its status changed significantly in 1951, when it was given the autonomy and new tools to oversee the country's macroeconomic policy. It was thus the period from the end of the Great Depression to the immediate postwar years that structured the Fed's public and macroeconomic role in the United States—a role that it still plays today. The objectives of full employment and price stability were not introduced in legislation until 1977, but in practice they were a part of the central bank's work much earlier.

The rejection of governmental influence on the central bank (thought to be one of the causes of inflation during the 1970s) and, crucially, the reemergence during the 1980s and 1990s of unbridled confidence in the self-regulation of financial markets partly overshadowed the integration of the central bank at the heart of the state. While the essential stabilizing role of central banks for the macroeconomy and public finances was not changed structurally, it was downplayed by an ideological discourse seeking to attribute to "the market" the virtues of an underlying social organization.

In reality, this period of financial liberalization did not end or even weaken the central banks' macroeconomic role. It was simply justified in a different way than it had been earlier. The legitimacy of the central banks' raisons d'être was never questioned, nor was the legitimacy of their interventions in the economy. The dominant economic theory of the 1980s and 1990s challenged the role of central banks in influencing the allocation of credit (credit policy) and in supporting industrial policy, but at the same time it also reinforced the received wisdom that central banks have better information in the macroeconomic domain than do private actors. As such, mainstream economic theory justified central banks' ability to dictate interest rates and thus to direct financial markets. The central banks remained powerful institutions, and, paradoxically, their power as economic stewards (and thus also their function as providers of insurance) increased apace. Financial markets were liberalized, financial institutions grew larger, and central banks grew more important and powerful.[17] This staying power, which is taken for granted today but was not a matter of course at the time, must be stressed. The management of the macroeconomic cycle by a public institution would have scandalized the free-market economists of the interwar period. To them, the function of a central bank was in principle limited to printing paper money backed by gold reserves. The central banks' macroeconomic omniscience was unquestioned during the period of deep and accelerating financial liberalization.[18]

The second half of the twentieth century thus established the central banks as the leading actors in formulating macroeconomic policy. They accompanied the transition from the Keynesian interventionist state of the postwar period to the neoliberal state starting in the 1980s. And their present development retains the characteristic features of neoliberalism: a growing reliance on market mechanisms and a presiding concern for private interests, but packaged as the decision-maker for (and with all the power of) the state in organizing markets and the economy.

The financial crisis of 2008, the European debt crisis that followed, and the COVID-19 pandemic highlighted the divine role of central banks, especially in their role as insurers, in the monetary system and in the state's financing. These crises showed the practical limits of faith in free-functioning financial markets while at the same time affirming the role of central banks as providential institutions seeking to maintain those markets' functioning. To understand the stakes involved in what happened, it is useful to imagine what the economy would be today had the central banks not assumed the role they did. What if, for example, central banks had responded in 2008 in the same way they responded to the Great Depression of the 1930s? It is impossible to understand modern central banks without going back to the sources of their fundamental transmutation in the middle of the twentieth century.

Following the financial crash of 1929, banking crises continued to occur, one after the other for a period of three years, in Europe and the United States. The difference then was that the central banks allowed the banks to go bankrupt because they believed that crisis was a necessary evil for an economy eroded by speculation and immorality. In some countries, such as Germany and Austria, this also led to a crisis of government debt. The social and political consequences elsewhere are also well documented, including economies devastated by deflation and unemployment, then by Nazism and war.[19]

By 2008 the central banks had grown to embody the role first entrusted to them sixty years earlier, when in the wake of World War II they were made integral components of the state in safeguarding employment and public credit. The central banks' interventions following the 2008 crisis thus served as a (belated) reminder of the total reimagining that these institutions had undergone—their integration into a state apparatus seeking to offer individuals protection against crises. But the financial system in the early twenty-first century was very different from the one that existed when central banks underwent wholesale changes and invented macroeconomic policy at the midpoint of the twentieth century. From the 1970s or 1980s onward—depending on the countries—financial institutions were increasingly privatized and financial practices liberalized. The imperatives for profit and the easing of regulation made financial institutions more leveraged and riskier. In the aftermath of this change, the question in 2008 was how the central bank's public role aligned with the private interests of the banking and financial sector; did the central banks save the people, or did the people save the banks?

Emphasizing the historical coincidence between the central banks' transition to public guardianship and the birth of the welfare state in the middle of the twentieth century is not to claim that central banks have since been mobilized to defend the welfare state or that they are not operating to defend the interests of private financial actors. If I stress this historical break, it is because the traditional history of monetary policy generally argues that the main turning point for central banks in the twentieth century occurred when they were granted full independence from governments during the 1980–1990s. I do not deny the existence of this second break, nor its effects and institutional persistence, but the interpretive framework that focuses on the independence of the central banks is not very useful for understanding the developments of monetary policy since the financial crisis of 2008–2009 (see chapters 3 and 4). Without appreciating the historical process of the integration of the central banks into the heart of the state, it is difficult to comprehend, for example, why the European Central Bank was created in the course of the 1990s with the goal of providing "support for the European Union's general economic policies"—that is, to support an economy that "aims at full employment and social progress, and a high level of protection and improvement of the quality of the environment" (see chapter 5). These words are not there by accident. And, even if they were underestimated during the first years of the European Central Bank, they were still not perceived as incompatible with the ECB's tenets of independence or its focus on price stability. They also would have been meaningless before the second half of the twentieth century.[20] For the same reasons, the objective of full employment included in the United States Federal Reserve Act since 1977 has not been erased.

"DECOMMODIFICATION"

The decisions made after 2008 (i.e., large-scale interventions by central banks in response to economic and financial crises) were unsurprising for anyone familiar with the social contract between central banks and states after World War II. But a narrower interpretation of the legal independence of the central banks, which had taken hold in most countries by the 1990s, had by then made it possible to see things differently. According to this erroneous interpretation, independence meant that the central bank could limit its activities to targeting inflation and that these activities would have no effect on the organization of financial markets or the management of government debt. This belief was based on an unshakable faith in the functioning of the liberal economic market—and forgetting that the historical role of a central bank was also to protect the state and society from the financial markets' errors and malfunctions.

The Danish sociologist Gøsta Esping-Andersen famously attributed a new characteristic to the concept of welfare state: decommodification.[21] Drawing on the works of the anthropologist and historian Karl Polanyi, Esping-Andersen centered decommodification on the ability of an institution (in this case, the state) to reduce individuals' dependence on, and vulnerability to, the forces of the economic market. The decommodifying forces in a society, then, are institutions like a public pension system, a public hospital, or education.

Attaching central banks to a theory of decommodification may appear paradoxical, even self-contradictory. Central banks, after all, intervene in financial markets, organize them, and in many ways defend the markets' raison d'être and interests.[22] But it is also true that the central banks' responsibilities include keeping society as a whole from suffering the kind of harmful effects of the market that would endanger financial and political stability. In this sense, central banks have deepened the role that Polanyi already attributed to them in the nineteenth century: "The need for protection arose from the way the money supply was organized in a market system. The modern Central Bank has indeed constituted a device intended to provide the protection, without which the market would have destroyed its own children."[23]

But decommodification is also a matter of degree, both as it relates to the central bank and to other sectors of the welfare state. According to Esping-Andersen, this degree of decommodification is in large measure what distinguishes the different types of welfare state (i.e., different proportions of state-controlled and market-controlled policies). Recent decades have shown that the welfare state can be undermined, even from within the state, by a countermovement toward commodifying public services—by drawing them away from the state and into market regulation. In the case of the central bank, the extent of decommodification itself depends on the extent of the financial system's liberalization— how regulated or unregulated the financial sector is—and thus on how (and how much) the central bank provides liquidity. The role of the central bank is to be a pillar of the financial system but not to independently define the function of finance in the economy.

The development of the central banks' characteristics over time, or their differences across countries, can be interpreted as an adaptation to changes in the nature of the banking and financial system and of the role of the state within it. If Chinese monetary policy in no way resembles the one we see in Europe, that is because the financial system and the state are organized in radically different ways.

Since the crisis of 2008, numerous critics have called for central banks to make fewer concessions to the interests of private financial institutions, or even to seek to replace the private institutions in certain cases, rather than simply safeguarding society against the harm these institutions can inflict. Today, this is a major issue that concerns economists, nongovernmental organizations, and political representatives interested in central banks. I shall return to this issue in my final chapter.

THE INSURANCE FUNCTION OF CENTRAL BANKS

In the domain of banking and finance, decommodification can move in various ways, depending on the choices made by governments—for example, the regulation of loans subsidized by public organizations or the regulation of interest rates. Decommodification of finance is therefore not principally the central bank's prerogative but rather something in which it participates (or doesn't) based on the state's choices regarding the organization of the financial system. It follows that the way in which the central bank operates actually depends on the degree and forms of government intervention in the financial system, as we shall see.

The central bank retains its agency through its unfettered ability to create money in order to provide liquidity for public or private institutions. The central bank's function of protection or insurance is thus centered on its ability to create liquidity. Since the unlimited provision of liquidity can produce harmful effects on an economy, the central bank has to make choices about when and how much to do so. Thus, the central bank's primary insurance function is necessarily political: it has to make choices that imply a definition of what constitutes the best functioning of its society, its financial system, and its state. Charles Goodhart said precisely this in his study of the functions of central banks: "With the Central Bank coming to represent the ultimate source of liquidity and support to the individual commercial banks, this micro function brought with it naturally a degree of 'insurance.' Such insurance, in turn, involves some risk of moral hazard."[24] This insurance function is not limited to making large loans to rescue banks in the event of a crisis (the central bank's celebrated status as "lender of last resort"). Every day, the central bank also provides liquidity by choosing the financial institutions that can benefit from it, including the types of loans (or the financial securities that serve to guarantee these loans) that those financial institutions make.

The history of central banks is rife with debates about the type of loans they can make and the effects of these choices on the economy. In the nineteenth century, for instance, the great debate concerned the appropriateness of making only short-term loans guaranteed by commercial transactions (*discount of bills of exchange*), or by making long-term loans guaranteed by real estate (mortgages). For a long time, most central banks refused to buy bonds on the financial markets that had been issued by companies or by the state because they viewed these purchases as an excessive intervention in those markets (or, perhaps, because these markets were not yet functional).[25] They preferred to lend only in response to the banks' requests (*standing facilities*).[26] In most countries (the United Kingdom and United States being exceptions), open-market operations (i.e., the purchase or sale of assets on the money market) became the norm only in the course of the financial liberalization of the 1980s and 1990s. Another salient example of the political and economic stakes involved in the central banks' choice of operations was the European Central Bank's decision to buy Greek debt after 2010 (see chapter 3).

The central bank's choice of where and how it exercises its powers thus reveals an overall political view of what the financial system ought to be. In each case, the terms of the debate are relatively similar—namely, whether the choice of new operations is a simple technical adjustment (in response to changes in the financial system) to strengthen the central bank's power, or whether the new financial instrument implies an insurance function and a quid pro quo with deeper and more political consequences. In the United States, for example, these debates concern the appropriateness of the Fed's purchase of corporate bonds.[27] In Japan or Europe, meanwhile, they concern loans granted by the central bank with conditions regarding how the money received by the companies is used (see chapters 3 and 4).

Contrary to what is sometimes thought, providing liquidity for financial institutions is not specific to central banks operating in liberalized financial systems. The basic techniques of central banks are surprisingly similar across financial systems, whether they are market-based (that is, free interest rates guide investors' arbitrages among different assets) or segmented (that is, there is no financial liberalization, interest rates play no role in asset allocation, and arbitrages among different types of assets are impossible). A central bank operating in a market-based system buys and sells tradeable assets, whereas a central bank in a segmented financial system (strongly monitored by the state) provides liquid assets principally in the form of direct short- or long-term loans to specific institutions. In both cases, the central bank provides liquidity, but the function of those liquid assets depends on the degree to which financial markets have been liberalized.

In a liberalized financial system, liquidity becomes a "global" rather than a "local" attribute: the central bank has no control over the final investment made by the institutions to which it makes loans. Transmission takes place through the market: the liquidity provided by the central bank can potentially lead to any kind of investment or speculation. This also means that the central bank ultimately becomes the guarantor of the market's functioning as a whole, including its potential for failure. This position predisposes it to buying the safest type of financial securities, both so that the market can profit from the safe asset and so that it can be exchanged by everyone. It is the function that American economist Perry Mehrling describes as "the dealer of last resort": the central bank intervenes in a way that establishes a reference price for a safe asset, which functions as a guarantee (or collateral) for the financial system's other exchanges.[28] By doing so, the central bank promotes stability in a liberalized market where stability is not a given.

On the other hand, when financial markets are segmented and thus isolated from one another (which includes the presence of capital controls, where foreign investment or capital inflows are limited by a government), liquidity becomes local: the central bank's supply of liquidity is no longer a support for the market as a whole, but for a specific type of economic activity whose financial solvency is deemed important to public welfare. Without rule of law and appropriate checks and balances, "local liquidity" can instead support private interests rather than a public objective.

The same distinction applies to public debt. The central bank can facilitate the financing of public debt by making direct loans to the state ("local" liquidity) or, on the contrary, by working through the market ("global" liquidity) to purchase it. It is easier to formulate conditions (quid pro quos) for loans when they are direct (to the state or to financial institutions) than when a central bank is purchasing securities on the open market. In the midst of recent crises, central bankers have rediscovered this principle as they hurry to purchase public debt. The insurance function of central banks operates through liquidity, but its goals are larger and multiple. The goal can be to absorb temporary, relatively minor financial shocks (for example, to even out the impact of seasonal variations) or to avoid major financial and economic crises.

The insurance contract between the central bank, the state, and the financial system is in large measure implicit, but it is above all "incomplete": it cannot foresee all contingencies. We cannot know in advance exactly what form the next financial crisis will take or what kind of asset the central bank should buy to limit its consequences. There are, of course, rules that guide the financial practices of central banks, and they are necessary. But it is impossible to determine ex ante every type of financial operations that they can carry out, and even less the exact conditions on which states and financial institutions can benefit from these operations.

THE ENGINE OF THE STATE

The relationship between the central bank and the financial system can be thought of as a push-pull along two axes.

First, the central bank aims to facilitate decommodification—to protect the state and the public from the natural whims and lesser impulses of financial markets. This is not a heresy, but to a certain extent an objective that is foundational to the central banks' actions, even if it is not always explicit. It was recognized by Polanyi's analysis mentioned above and confirmed by numerous studies on the history of central banks.

Second, central banks seek to meet the objectives that society assigns them by guaranteeing the proper functioning of the banking and financial systems. One critical component of this is making sure that the banking and financial systems are allowed to exist. If central banks had to circumvent or replace the financial system as a whole, they would lose their purpose. Equally, the role a democratic society assigns to its central bank is deeply connected with the way that society views financial markets, their role, and their regulation. The identities of the central bank and the financial system thus both mutually uphold and reflect the societies they serve.

The movements of central banks along each of these axes can appear ambiguous, even contradictory. On the one hand, central banks function as substitutes for banks and other financial institutions when the latter produce instability; on the other hand, they help strengthen the infrastructures of financial markets to ensure their functioning in normal times. They grease the wheels of financial intermediation; they also protect it from mechanical overheating. These different interventional poles reflect the development of central banks over time: they have been historically linked to states' wills to develop and shape credit markets, and those states have exhibited differing degrees of liberalism across time and place.

In many countries, and from their earliest days, central banks have had the objective—in addition to issuing money and ensuring the stability of the payment system—of unifying the credit market or making the public debt market functional and liquid. Unifying the credit market at the national level was done by installing branches of the central bank throughout the country so that banks and companies everywhere would have access to loans on the same conditions.[29] The central bank lent in certain regions at interest rates below the market rate, so that the conditions of access to credit became uniform at the national level. It therefore initially replaced the market at the local level, but this substitution had the goal of allowing the development of a market throughout the country. This guarantee worked not only in the event of a financial crisis but, more generally, whenever demand for credit required it and risked exceeding supply, such as during seasonal fluctuations linked to agriculture or when international interest rates changed. Thus, the cost of not having a central bank became too great for a country seeking to develop economically and integrate into international financial markets. Because of its lack of a central bank before 1913, the United States was much more exposed to international financial upheavals than comparable countries. When the Bank of England—at the time the most influential central bank in the world—raised its interest rate, the consequences for interest rates and financial markets in the United States were three times greater than elsewhere.[30] The creation of the Federal Reserve was not only a solution to this problem for the United States; it also made it possible to encourage the use of the dollar internationally after World War I because of its insurance function for worldwide dollar loans.[31] It was therefore both the protective role of the state and its economic and geopolitical power that were embodied in this new institution, as had been the case for European countries from the nineteenth century onward.

But the historical role of the central bank was not limited to unifying interest rates on business loans and to developing financial markets under the impetus of the state. The state also had to be able to finance itself. Making the public debt market functional and liquid involved the central bank buying public debt, accepting public debt as a guarantee for loans, and even sometimes taking part in the sale of this debt to private individuals or to banks on behalf of the state. The central bank however remains a bank, that is an entity that is distinct from the Treasury department. At the end of the eighteenth century, Adam Smith said of the Bank of England: "It acts not only like an ordinary bank, but also like a great engine of state."[32]

THE CENTRAL BANK VERSUS THE PUBLIC INVESTMENT BANK

Here the major difference between a central bank and a public investment bank (also called public development or promotional bank) must be emphasized. Recent events and the financial influence acquired by central banks may contribute to confusion between these two types of institutions; their respective roles and functions warrant clarification in order to understand the finer points of the possible role to be played by central banks in the ecological transition.

A public investment bank (like the Caisse des dépôts or the Banque publique d'investissement in France, and the European Investment Bank in Europe) is created by the state, with its guarantee, and with the goal of promoting long-term loans to companies and municipalities at interest rates lower than the market rate.[33] These long-term loans usually finance infrastructure or investments in real estate (especially for agriculture and social housing). Central banks and public investment banks have in common that they are the strong arm of the state in the financial sector. In many countries, they have a joint history, having been established at the same time and often maintaining financial and political connections with one another.

Here, however, their primary goals diverge. As we have emphasized, a central bank must ensure the proper functioning of the monetary system and of lending, while avoiding financial or inflationary crises. A public investment bank aims to invest over the long term in sectors that the state considers to have a high priority. It cannot create money, and it is generally financed by long-term bonds, or in some cases, by regulated deposits, like the Caisse des dépôts in France, which manages regulated deposits that are collected by private banks but whose interest rate and ceilings are set by the state (*livret A*). *Livret A* deposits are used by the Caisse des dépôts exclusively to finance social housing.

In the course of history, central banks have provided financial support—with short- or medium-term loans—to public investment banks. Even today, the latter can borrow from the European

Central Bank, for example. In China, these two types of institutions are highly integrated.[34] But the difference between the central bank and public investment banks remains. In Europe that difference is one of the essential conditions of the independence of both institutions (see chapter 4). The public investment banks of European countries and the European Investment Bank are also independent by law; they cannot take orders from the government or finance the state budget. However, they are more closely regulated by parliaments than central banks. Parliaments are usually represented on their supervisory boards, even when this is not a form of direct control. The United States is a notable exception because it does not have a large public investment bank. Instead, it has government-sponsored enterprises that play a key role in mortgage finance.

A financial system is thus composed of private institutions (banks or investment funds), the public treasury (which issues public debt), public investment banks (which provide long-term financing in accord with the state's priorities while being independent from the government), and a central bank whose principal role is to maintain the stability of the entire system. Any attempt to think about one of these institutions in isolation from the others is pointless. Articulating the connection between the regulation of *private* financial institutions and the management of *public* financial institutions (the central bank, public investment banks, and the public treasury) is a domain called credit policy (see chapter 4).

THE WELFARE STATE AND THE ECOLOGICAL TRANSITION

The central bank is thus a pillar of the welfare state in the sense that it provides a kind of insurance—and with it, a kind of decommodification—that ensures the protection of citizens, all of whom face economic risks. It merits repeating: this decommod-ification is only a matter of degree. The same operation by a central bank—supplying liquidity—can be a means for insulating citizens from market failures or, on the contrary, can promote financial development or even speculation.[35] From this arises a fundamen-tal democratic question: Who should decide—and how—what the degree is?

This question becomes all the more important if we follow Esping-Andersen, who tells us that another role of the modern welfare state is to provide insurance that permits the economy to achieve a transition. Writing in the 1990s, Esping-Andersen believed that this transition was from an essentially industrial economy to a service economy. Today, the same line of reasoning can be applied to the transition toward an economy that respects the environment. The role of the welfare state in the ecological transition is justified by a dynamic, not static, view of the welfare state's insurance function: investing and regulating today to avoid paying damages tomorrow. As I will show in chapter 4, central banks can now take part in this function, which is indispensable for the ecological transition.

Raising questions of monetary policy in the context of future environmental calamity may strike some as abstraction. But from a political perspective, its relevance and importance are evident in light of the central bank's protective role in a medium- and long-term perspective: the central bank's liquidity today must help protect society from risks tomorrow. And tomorrow's macro-economic risks may endanger the value of money and financial stability. Today, the risk is principally climate, which is why the law of the European Union requires the ECB to provide support for environmental policies.

Asking these questions must not lead to thinking that the ECB can and must do everything—that it is the maker of future providence. Instead, we have to reason in terms of the financial system we have, including its constraints, and clearly define the place of the central bank within it, an important but not ubiquitous place. To understand this, let us now turn, in concrete terms, to the way in which central banks create money and act on the economy.

Money from Nowhere

Despite the great complexity of the institution's operations, the term *central bank* is surprisingly literal. It is a "bank" in the sense that its main activity is to lend money. It is "central" in the sense that it serves as an intermediary through which other banks may interact, both on an everyday basis and in times of crisis. By understanding this centrality within the banking system, we can understand the way money is created today and the political and financial stakes tied up in the process.

HOW A CENTRAL BANK CREATES MONEY

A central bank has two main ways of intervening in the financial market: buying (or selling) financial securities, and lending to financial institutions (mostly banks). In the first case, it chooses the market in which it intervenes (and thus the type of financial security that it buys, whether public debt or a company's private debt). In the second case, it promises banks that it can lend to them at a certain rate of interest on the condition that they provide a financial guarantee as collateral.[1] In that case, the central bank does not buy the security but retains it as a guarantee until the bank repays the loan. To buy or lend financial securities, the central bank creates money; that is, the money that it lends did not exist beforehand.

Through these two types of interventions, the central bank can control the price of credit—the interest rate offered by banks—throughout the economy. When it modifies the rates of interest at which it lends, the central bank also adjusts its lending and its purchases of securities. In normal times, the central bank does not need to lend much to banks in order to ensure that the interest rate for bank lending in the economy is close to the rate at which the central bank lends. But during a financial crisis, or when its interest rate is already very low (fig. 1), it has to increase its interventions sharply.

For these reasons, central banks have created enormous amounts of money since the financial crisis of 2008; the amount of money created by the European Central Bank and the Federal Reserve increased sevenfold between 2007 and 2021 (fig. 2).

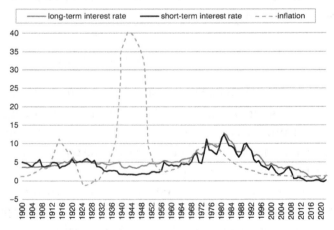

FIGURE 1 The central bank's interest rate, the long-term interest rate on public debt, and the rate of inflation averaged (in percent, 1900–2021) for the US, UK, Japan, France, Germany, and Italy

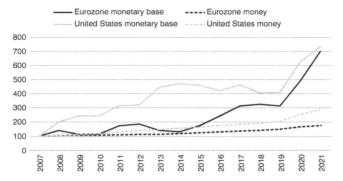

FIGURE 2 Comparative evolution of the monetary base and money in the eurozone and the United States, 2007–2021 (index 2007 =100)

Note: The *monetary base* is defined as the money created directly by the central bank (banknotes and private banks' deposits in the central bank) as for a counterpart of its operations. *Money* is the monetary supply, including deposits in banks by private individuals and businesses (M2). The series have been adjusted so that their value in 2007 is equal to 100. Thus, the graph shows that the United States' monetary base increased by a factor of 4 between 2007 and 2018 (the index rose by 100 to 406), whereas money increased by a factor of 2.

This observation raises three questions: Why didn't this period of extraordinary monetary creation automatically generate a strong rise in the rate of inflation long before the end of the COVID-19 pandemic, especially since public consensus held that the rise in the quantity of money made prices increase? Second, why didn't the increase in the quantity of money created by the central bank (i.e., the monetary base) result in an equivalent increase in the amount of money circulating in the economy (i.e., the money supply)? Finally, where did this money go, and why was it necessary to create so much of it? Answering these questions requires going into the details of the action of central banks, but this is essential to understanding the functioning of the financial system and the role of central banks within it.

When the central bank lends to a private bank or purchases a

TABLE 1. The central bank's simplified balance sheet

Assets	Liabilities
Loans made to banks	Money in circulation (coins and bills)
Domestic financial securities (including public debt)	Deposits held by banks (i.e., obligatory reserves + excess reserves)
Foreign exchange reserves (international securities)	Equity

financial security, it creates money; it increases its liabilities. The money created by the central bank—coins and bills, as well as private banks' deposits in the central bank—appears on the liability side of table 1. Unless a special law limits this creation (as has happened in history), the central bank can create as much money as it likes.[2]

This is not all that different from the activities of a private bank, which can also create money by lending. All a private bank has to do is create deposits corresponding to the amount of the loan—a simple accounting operation. But central banks retain the privilege of issuing banknotes, and in this and other activities they are subject to less regulation than private banks. Private banks are in fact required to hold capital proportionate to the deposits they create or to the amount on their balance sheet. The central bank also has no private creditors that could force it into bankruptcy if it suffers losses, as it will still be able to repay its debts by printing banknotes that are legal tender or can be recapitalized by the government.

In practice—especially today—the central bank's liabilities are increased not just by printing banknotes but also by crediting the private banks' accounts (that is, by increasing their deposits) at the central bank. If the central bank buys or lends a hundred dollars to a bank, that means that the amount in this bank's account at the central bank is increased by a hundred dollars. This same bank can do what it wants with this money, but no matter how it uses it, this money will always be transferred to another bank—specifically, to the private bank's account at the central bank. Thus, banks trade with each other, but the total amount of the central bank's reserves remains stable.[3]

In other words, the central bank creates money when it buys a financial security (for example, a public debt) from a bank or lends that bank money. But that money takes the form of a deposit in the central bank, and this deposit (also called a "reserve") is a particular form of money that banks exchange between themselves by means of transfers between their accounts in the central bank. Thus, deposits in the central bank can diminish only if the central bank sells financial securities (or does not renew loans that have reached their maturity date), or if a commercial bank decides to ask that its deposits in the central bank be exchanged for bank notes. But these exchanges for bank notes concern relatively small amounts. In normal times, the money the central bank creates for banks does not circulate among individuals as cash but allows banks to carry on their activities and thus, ultimately, to make loans and payments.

SAFE ASSETS AND RISKY ASSETS

Economists long thought that banks automatically increased their loans in proportion to the reserves that they held in the central bank—that more reserves meant more money in circulation. This is the theory of the *money multiplier*, the foundation of monetarism that was popularized by Milton Friedman and the Chicago School of Economics in the twentieth century. This view is particularly erroneous in the current system, where private banks are financed more by borrowing on the financial markets than by individuals' deposits. It is clear that the consequences of the monetary policy pursued since 2008 invalidate the theory of Friedman and the monetarists: The money created by the central bank (the "monetary base") has increased enormously, but the overall money supply (including deposits made in banks by businesses and individuals) and bank credits have, for their part, increased much more modestly (see fig. 2). The return of inflation since 2021 cannot be attributed to the direct consequences of monetary policy since 2008, even though the low level of interest rates may have contributed to a rapid resumption of demand after the end of the COVID-19 pandemic. Outside the United States and United Kingdom, salaries have increased little, and the rise of prices has been driven mainly by energy costs. Within the eurozone, rates of inflation diverge greatly from one country to the next, without any connection to the differing trajectories of monetary creation. If money rose sharply during the COVID-19 pandemic, preceding the return of high inflation rates, it was not only because of central bank and government support but also because households accumulated savings in bank accounts. They spent this money once the lockdowns were over, pushing up prices. Inflation, we see, is not directly tied to the amount of money created by the central bank.

The disconnect between money created by the central bank and inflation reflects the nature of the present financial system. In the course of the 2000s, the banking and financial system of wealthy countries reached an unprecedented scale of development and size (especially as a proportion of national income).[4] The paradox of this system—and it has only grown since the crisis of 2008—is that it needs safety to function. To lend money to businesses or to households, banks now have to hold in parallel a larger volume of safe assets than they did earlier. Thus, there is a very strong demand for assets that are very secure and very liquid (i.e., assets that can be easily sold), like money.

Accordingly, the real rate of interest on these assets—in particular, public debt—is very low (as seen in figure 1). The central banks themselves seek to maintain these low rates and, if necessary, to buy public debt in order to do so. By purchasing public or private debt, central banks create reserves for the banks, and this form of money functions as a safe asset, which in turn functions as a base for the liquidity of the financial system.[5] Before the return of inflation in 2022 and the rise in interest rates, these reserves weren't lucrative—the central bank remunerated them at a negative interest rate, meaning that it cost private banks money to maintain them. This would seemingly compel private banks to turn to riskier and potentially more profitable assets. Certainly, some did. But the strong demand for safe assets was equally tenacious and persistent. In wealthy countries, the real yield on safe assets remains low when inflation rises.

Many factors have contributed to the growing demand for low-risk or risk-free assets: the liberalization of the flow of capital globally; the privatization of finance; and the privatization of certain sectors of the economy (such as retirement pensions and education), as well as the growth of overall wealth and of inequalities in capital ownership, are just a few. Overall, the sheer volume of private savings to be managed is enormous, and financial flows have mushroomed as financial liberalization has stimulated the pursuit of cash assets and gains. This increase in private savings—which is consistent with the growth of capital relative to wage earnings, as diagnosed by Thomas Piketty[6]—is the result of several converging trends: inequalities that favor the accumulation of savings by a small number of people; the fact that societies are getting both wealthier and older; and the increasing privatization of retirement systems.

Thus, central banks' growing balance sheets as a percentage of GDPs have reached a historically exceptional level (see fig. 3 in the next chapter). But that is not the case for the ratio between the central bank's balance sheet and the size of the financial system. It is very difficult to propose an exact measure of the size of the financial sector, but it is indisputable that it is, like the balance sheets of the central banks, at its highest historical level relative to GDP. As the world has become more financialized, central banks have grown. This relationship, historians and economists have shown, has been consistent across recent history.[7]

SHOULD RISK BE REINJECTED INTO THE ECONOMY?

The central bank's balance sheet, with its credit (public debt) and its liability (the banks' reserves), is thus the heart of the financial system, where a balance between the interests of states and those of banks is constructed and monitored. The central bank absorbs this system's risk. This balance, which is today more or less stable in spite of everything, has no doubt made it possible to avoid the collapse of financial systems and economic activity in wealthy countries, particularly in Europe, the United States, and Japan.

Nonetheless, it raises many questions that go far beyond the role of the central bank and also challenge the intrinsic logic of this system. By absorbing in large measure the financial risk, the central banks contribute—through a domino effect—to raising the price of all assets that involve no risk (e.g., public debt, real estate, and certain stocks or bonds). (The price of an asset is inversely correlated with its return—the interest rate.) The central bank's purchases of assets and its lowering of interest rates are thus two sides of the same coin: these actions increase the value of capital, but they potentially increase wealth inequalities as well. In addition, causing the price of public debt to fall can lead governments to go into debt rather than seek different ways of financing the state's budget, in particular through the tax system.

Second, policymakers are increasingly asking whether it is necessary to reinject a certain form of risk into the economy, notably by financing long-term projects whose profitability is uncertain. This question is raised particularly with regard to the financing necessary for the ecological transition. But it cannot be achieved by central banks alone. Since the central bank's asset-purchase programs mainly allow governments to take on long-term, low-cost debt, the onus is now largely on governments to support very long-term investments that the market considers too risky to render as stable assets.

Third, there is evidence that low rates of interest and central banks' policies of absorbing risk in the 2010s in fact led some financial actors to take more risks to seek a greater return. The rise of the price of certain risky stocks, or even cryptocurrencies such as Bitcoin, may testify to this trend. However, although this effect seems for the moment to be weak, it is necessary to make sure that the central banks' policy does not consist in an excessive relocation and concentration of risk-taking toward fragile, speculative, or counterproductive investments.[8]

In the eyes of the general public, the central banks' policy from 2008 to 2021 has had the advantage of making it easier to take out loans. Those who borrow—including states—are delighted by the low rates. Those who save are, on the contrary, dismayed to see their financial holdings valued at a rate lower than that of inflation, without necessarily understanding that these low rates are the counterpart of rescuing the financial capitalism that allows them to save in this very way.

Recent criticisms of central banks rightly stress the fact that their large asset purchases increase wealth inequality, encourage the development of shadow banking, and incentivize governments to borrow rather than to tax. But it is not for central banks to decide to change the financial system, at least not independent of government policies and democratic choices. Proposals to reform financial systems are numerous. A tax on capital, for instance, would reduce the public debt and society's inequalities of wealth. A public pension scheme diminishes private savings (and thus the role of large asset managers) and inequalities, in contrast to a retirement system based on financialization. Regulated savings (such as the "livret A" in France, intended to finance social housing) can be directed toward long-term investment without the need to resort to short-term loans on the financial markets, etc. Amid criticisms of the excessive size of the financial system and the public debt, an eye could productively be turned toward reforms of this kind rather than considering the central bank's operations in isolation. Yet, central banks and parliaments should take into account criticisms and contemplate alternative monetary policy instruments that minimize side effects and are consistent with a broader credit policy of the state (chapters 4 and 5).

CAN A CENTRAL BANK GO BANKRUPT?

A central bank can suffer losses on each of its types of assets (table 1). Thus, losses can result from a default in the financial securities that it holds (for example, if a state can no longer pay back its debts), a default of the banks or enterprises to which the central bank has lent directly, or a loss of value in foreign exchange reserves. In practice, the last case—tanking foreign exchange reserves—is the most frequent. It can result from the devaluation of a foreign currency that the central banks hold as reserve; this was the case, for example, for countries that held the pound sterling in 1931 or 1967, or for those that held dollars in 1971 and 1973. More generally, in a flexible system of exchange rates, an increase in the value of the domestic currency creates losses for central banks. In history, and still today for most countries (in particular in emerging markets that try to maintain a stable rate of exchange), international reserves often constitute most of the central bank's balance sheet. And, contrary to domestic financial securities, the central banks register in their account the price of foreign financial securities at the present market value—not at the book value. This explains why the losses result for the most part from fluctuations in the value of foreign exchange reserves.

Another potential source of losses is financial crisis. The central bank's role as lender of last resort can produce losses if the private banks end up going bankrupt or if loan collateral proves insufficient. The largest central banks avoided this type of loss during the crisis of 2008–2009,[9] due in part to the fact that they accepted financial securities of good quality as guarantees for loans that they made but also to the fact that they acted in parallel to ensure the liquidity of these guarantees; this was particularly the case with public debt, of which the central banks purchased plenty in the aftermath of the crisis. If a country had defaulted on its public debt in the midst of the financial crisis, these central banks would most certainly have suffered losses. The central banks also created structural barriers to losses during the crisis, creating "resolution mechanisms" to organize the bankruptcies or the restructurings of certain banks or financial institutions in such a way as to ensure that bank shareholders or states incurred the risk, not the central banks themselves.[10]

A final variable in the finances of a central bank is the difference between the rate of interest on the loans that it makes (or equally, the remuneration of the assets that it buys) and the rate at which it remunerates the bank deposits that it receives. This is a relatively new challenge, historically. It was only at the beginning of the 2000s that central banks started to remunerate bank reserves. The restrictive monetary policies of the 1980s to combat inflation involved an increase in lending rates but not in the remuneration of bank reserves at the central bank.

A central bank can therefore have losses, like any financial institution. But does that mean that it can go bankrupt? The answer has been no for some time—more or less since central banks stopped having private shareholders with control over the institution.[11] But broadly, and structurally, the liabilities of a central bank are not comparable to those of a private bank because, in reality, the central bank doesn't owe anything to anyone. In fact, a central bank can even maintain negative equity—with its liabilities exceeding its assets—without a loss of its core institutional functions. This is not to say that banks or governments find negative equity appealing; most would rather avoid it. Central banks are often reluctant to have negative equity over a long period, and in these situations, governments may recapitalize the central bank.[12] The other way to avoid negative equity is to create new money to compensate for losses.[13]

Not having to worry about potential losses is a defining strength of central banks and a core element of their insurance function—the absorption of risk. A central bank's ability to lend in times of crisis while also creating money to guarantee the liquidity and the safety of assets in the economy is based on the central bank's insensitivity to financial losses, a luxury that private banks don't have. Thus—and this may seem paradoxical—it is because the central bank is less sensitive to losses than a commercial bank that the central bank ultimately does not suffer losses.

The financial independence of central banks is also considered a kind of guarantee of their operational independence—the trait that ostensibly makes them above acting in self-interest.[14] If central banks had to make a fixed annual payment to their shareholders (including the state), or if they had constraints on their capital, they could lose flexibility, which would risk damaging their credibility with respect to their insurance role.

This does not mean that the finances of a central bank are not an appropriate subject of public debate or parliamentary control.

Ultimately, the state is the central bank's shareholder—the party that receives dividends in the event of profits and that, alternatively, receives nothing or recapitalizes in case of losses.[15] It would be counterproductive for a state to force a central bank to make profits. But it is not unreasonable for the state to be concerned about how the central bank is managed, since the choices the bank makes always ultimately imply financial transfers. When the central bank makes losses, the state no longer receives dividends. And the central bank's losses may be due to questionable investment strategies or interest rate policies. Central bank finances therefore warrant public debate and parliamentary oversight. In countries like China or Switzerland, where the central bank holds enormous amounts of foreign currencies in order to avoid an excessive appreciation of the exchange rate, the question arises—and has often been posed publicly in the case of Switzerland—of whether it is appropriate to remunerate so many states and foreign companies in this way and to incur losses because of the evolution of the exchange rate over time.[16] The remuneration of commercial banks' deposits in the central bank also raises questions regarding the justification of such a financial transfer to these banks. This conversation will return and escalate as the central banks raise their interest rates and pay more for private banks' deposits. In these cases, the question becomes whether the central bank's operations and instruments are really suited to its objectives—and who benefits directly from the power of monetary creation.

CAN THE CENTRAL BANK FINANCE EVERYTHING?

Every discussion of monetary creation inevitably raises the question of its limits. Why don't central banks finance all investment or public expenditures? I cannot explore the whole range of the answers to this question, which has divided economists for centuries, but it does seem to me that it can be answered broadly on the basis of a few simple intuitions.

Free-market economists believe that in order to let the market function freely, the central bank's adventures in the economy should be centered solely on interest rates—and that central banks should neither replace commercial banks in the granting and allocation of credit nor provide guidance to them.[17] But there are also two opposing arguments on this matter. The first argument cites situations in which it is recognized that the state must spend more to support economic activity, maintain financial stability, and avoid deflation, and in these special cases the central bank is the only institution capable of lending it sufficient resources at no interest or at a moderate rate of interest. The second argument cites the fact that the financial and banking markets may function in a silo—that is, in a compartmentalized or segmented manner—that is far from the ideal of perfect market competition. In this view, some sectors are underfinanced, while others, on the contrary, are sites of speculative bubbles. The state can either try to organize this compartmentalized financial activity, typically in cooperation with a broader industrial policy that seeks to support targeted market sectors (as was the case in Europe before the 1980s or presently in China), or it can try to reform the banking system to break down these silos within the economy, even though some of them may remain because of the markets' intrinsic dysfunctions. The central bank adapts to these landscapes by modulating its volumes and conditions for loans depending on the sectors or types of credit. This may be a matter of macroprudential policy (to preserve financial stability), of loans to targeted banks under certain conditions, or even of direct loans to businesses. All these solutions have been tried in the past. The question is whether the central bank is the most suitable institution to make choices concerning the allocation of credit.

According to standard macroeconomic arguments, the central bank is justified in increasing its loans or asset purchases so long as inflation and economic activity are considered too weak to guarantee the well-being of the population—and so long as there is room for the central bank to effect positive economic change. This occurs especially when nominal interest rates are at the zero lower bound. This principle was applied after the 2008 financial crisis and during the recent pandemic. The work of democratic and economic debate, then, is to determine when the side effects of such policies (on inflation, financial stability, inequality, etc.) exceed their expected gains.

Thus, the central bank's creation of money can run up against two types of limits. The first is a macroeconomic limit, which is defined principally by inflation and financial stability: creating money can cause an increase of prices and of speculation if it exceeds the real demand needed to finance production and consumption. The second limit is political, and determining this limit requires an honest analysis and discussion of the economic effectiveness and democratic framework of the central bank—a process similar to that accompanying any other state intervention.

Is the central bank in the best position to choose to whom loans should be made, according to what criteria, and in what amounts? Would a public investment bank be better situated to make such choices? How can societies proceed so that the process of monetary creation occurs in accordance with transparent principles of economic efficacy, and not for reasons of special interest or regulatory capture? Wouldn't a system of progressive taxes (that is, a contribution according to revenues or capital) offer a more equitable and transparent approach to financing the public debt, or at least one better than money creation? If the central bank funds the government directly until inflation forces the central bank to restrict that funding—as the relationship has been theorized by the school of thought known as modern monetary theory—then we have only shifted these questions toward another question: that of the power and legitimacy of the state budget. And it is not clear that the transparency of allocation choices has increased along the way. Monetary creation is often discussed in a mystical or excessively theoretical way. At the risk of disappointing the reader, a more realistic approach to monetary policy would be centered on the oldest question in economic policy: Should the economy be organized in a centralized manner defined by the public power, or in a decentralized way, through market mechanisms? Is there a middle ground? The role assigned to the central bank depends on one's answer to that question.

FINANCIAL STABILITY: AN EXPLICIT OBJECTIVE?

The objective of financial stability often remains implicit in the mandate of central banks, even if it is essential in practice. It can be defined as the ability to avoid a crisis of the financial intermediaries (including banks) and to ensure that they are on the whole capable of lending and repaying what they have borrowed. Before the 2008 crisis, many economists believed that the stability of consumer prices was a sufficient guarantee of financial stability; this theory is obviously no longer viable. Today, financial stability is recognized as an objective in its own right, but one that remains implicit: it is presented as a condition of the stability of prices, of the stability of the system of payment, and of the proper conduct of monetary policy.

There are two reasons why financial stability does not generally appear as an explicit objective of the central bank. First, it is not the only institution that has a duty to ensure financial stability. Regulators and supervisors of banks, stock markets, the insurance sector, and consumer protection are also stakeholders in this cause, and each has its own domain. Second, financial stability is hard to define. Stock prices, for example, rise and fall, but their fluctuations seldom have major consequences for the real economy. Nor does a bank's failure necessarily lead to larger financial instability. Thus, there are good reasons why financial stability continues to be vaguely and contextually defined. It remains an implicit objective—a means of achieving the more explicit goals held closely by central banks.

After the 2008 crisis, governments established a new type of policy and an institution to guarantee financial stability: the macroprudential policy. Its objective was, and remains, to avoid a banking or financial crisis by monitoring the debt of households and businesses, whether financial or nonfinancial. As such, macroprudential policy deals with economic issues that are outside the remit of central banks.

Accordingly, macroprudential policy is not overseen by the central bank alone, and central banks are not the only institutions that have a responsibility to monitor financial stability (see chapter 4). Even so, it remains that the existence of banking regulation or, more recently, a macroprudential policy does not change one of the essential roles played by the central bank: ensuring monetary and financial stability by granting loans to banks and other agencies. In this regard, their core function remains unchanged, if still largely unwritten.

More Problems

Buying Debt, Lending Abroad,
and Going Digital

The central bank's two types of economic interventions—purchasing financial securities or extending loans—offer an infinite range of possibilities. Since the 2008 crisis, central banks have broadly diversified and increased their operations relative to what they were at the beginning of the century, marking a return to the complex practices and instruments mastered in the years between 1950 and 1980 but which had fallen partly into disuse in the course of the 1990s.

This inventiveness contributed to a considerable upward trend in the complexity of central bank policies, a trend that does not seem likely to disappear any time soon. It has also produced a drastic augmentation of the central banks' actual financial operations, and thus of the size of their balance sheets, to amounts unprecedented in times of peace.

During the 1990s and at the beginning of the twenty-first century (before the 2008 crisis), the central banks of wealthy economies decreased the size and the complexity of their interventions for two reasons. First, these major economies had abandoned their objectives of fixed exchange rates. As a result, the central banks no longer needed to buy and sell international financial securities (called "foreign exchange reserves") to stabilize their exchange rates. Second, it had become accepted that the independence of the central banks had to be accompanied by their minimal interventions in the markets (besides setting interest rates) in order to avoid hindering those markets' function. This idea was based on a belief in the virtues of markets—a core driver of the financial liberalization of the period that this book has referenced repeatedly—as well as the principle according to which the central bank's independence could be called into question if its interventions entailed choices that were deemed too consequential in political terms (by favoring this or that financial security or this or that sector, for example).[1] Third, the relatively fluid functioning of the interbank market and the limited impact (at the time) of financial crises allowed the central banks of the wealthiest countries to reach the desired level of interest rates without resorting to extensive, complex interventions. In essence, the stability of the period fostered a belief that crises were a thing of the past. In the early 2000s, several economists even thought that in the future the central banks might base their policies solely on communication, without needing to buy financial securities or lend to banks.[2]

This idea was demolished by the central banks' reaction to the financial crisis of 2008 and to the economic crisis that followed. Marking the break from the preceding period of relative nonintervention, the central banks suddenly described their policies as "nonconventional." Today, we can confidently characterize these "nonconventional" policies as having become deeply conventional.

The successive crises of the twenty-first century have been occasionally linked in the public memory, but it is useful to distinguish them. In each case, the central banks had to respond to distinct problems, problems that required new and unusual interventions. First there was the global crisis of 2008–2009, which was simultaneously a financial, banking, economic, and international crisis. Then between 2010 and 2012, a public debt crisis struck the European Union, followed by a low rate of inflation and a high rate of unemployment. The crisis provoked by the COVID-19 pandemic and its ensuing high inflation followed in 2020 and 2021. The war in Ukraine constituted a further crisis, one whose monetary consequences will be felt for years to come.

PURCHASES OF PUBLIC DEBT

Amid the relative stability of 2019, some predicted that the global financial system would gradually return to the "normal" landscape of pre-2008. This fanciful notion was quickly dispelled by the COVID-19 crisis, which amplified the trend toward chaos established during the preceding decade. In the eurozone, the "pandemic emergency purchase programme (PEPP)" established by the ECB led the central bank to take on even more debt, including the purchase of three-quarters of the total public debt issued by countries in the eurozone since the beginning of the pandemic.

The ECB's balance sheet rose beyond 50 percent of the eurozone's GDP (see figure 3), and over time the ECB took on almost a quarter of each European country's stock of public debt (see figure 4). By way of comparison and example, these amounts are historically unprecedented in Europe in peacetime. The situation was similar in other economically developed countries (the United Kingdom, Sweden, the United States) and reached its extreme in Japan, where the central bank's balance sheet grew to exceed the country's GDP, with the central bank holding more than half the country's public debt.

These unprecedented numbers raise questions because the current definition of central bank independence means that they are not supposed to lend directly to governments.[3] For example, the Eurosystem, comprising the ECB and the central banks of EU member states, is barred under article 123 of the Treaty on

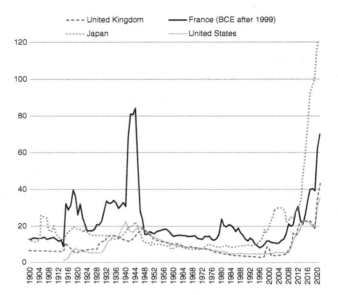

FIGURE 3 The central banks' balance sheet as a percentage of GDP, 1900–2021

Note: The United States' central bank was not created until 1913. The balance sheet of the Banque de France was used from 1900 to 1998 and then replaced by that of the ECB (as a percentage of the eurozone's GDP). The trend is similar if we look at other large countries in the eurozone.

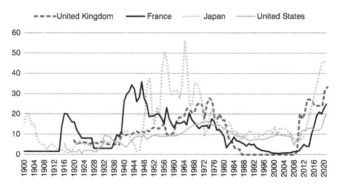

FIGURE 4 Public debt held by central banks as a percentage of the total public debt, 1900–2020

Note: The United States created its central bank only in 1913. After 1998, the graph shows the French public debt held by the Banque de France (on behalf of the Eurosystem). This trend is similar to that in other countries of the eurozone.

the Functioning of the European Union from granting "overdraft facilities or any other type of credit facility" directly to member states. This means that the central banks' acquisition of public debt has to occur indirectly—purchased from private banks and under the guise of monetary policy. This lacks historical precedent. Compared to times of war or to the 1950s and 1960s, when the central banks held, on average, 20 percent of the public debt, today's central bank balance sheets are larger than ever before— and seemingly accompanied by no real recognition of this fact or of a contract between the government and the central bank specifying the way in which public debt is to be managed. In France, during the postwar period, the government voted for a limit on how much public debt could be financed by the Banque de France. (By law, this limit remained in force until 1993, even though by then the Banque de France held no more than 3 percent of total public debt.)[4]

Paradoxically, the central banks' independence thus allowed them to buy public debt with less political constraint than when they were less independent at earlier stages of history. It is nonetheless unlikely that the ECB can continue to hold and buy so much public debt without ultimately embarking on a coordination between monetary policy, which the central bank oversees, and fiscal policy, which the government oversees. Failing that, the governments of the eurozone would potentially be at the mercy of when and under what circumstances the central bank elected to resell part of its debt assets. If the ECB decided to keep this public debt, it would have to justify doing so by pointing out that selling it would lead to a rise in interest rates, which could in turn destabilize the governments of the eurozone.

Any such outwardly political motive for how the ECB regards its balance sheet would be historically and politically significant—a gesture tantamount to acknowledging that the definition of financial stability is in fact dependent on the mode in which the public debt of the states is financed (i.e., by central banks or by private financial institutions). While this debate may be necessary and overdue, it does not exist in a vacuum; the political and legal tensions that have punctuated the ECB's purchases of public debt since 2012 make proceeding with it challenging for both sides.

Unlike the central banks of the United States or England in particular, the Eurosystem initially reacted to the crisis of 2008 by lending to banks rather than by buying financial securities on the markets. Historically, loans to banks have had a greater impact on the practices of the central banks in continental Europe than elsewhere, making these kinds of loans more ingrained in the Eurosystem's habits. In addition, the eurozone differed from individual countries in that it had no common public debt, which in an emergency would have created barriers to agreements regarding how to buy public debt.

That was how the Eurosystem confronted the crisis of European public debt in 2010–2012: When it made a loan to a private bank, the central bank accepted the public bonds issued by the country in crisis (in particular, Greek debt) as guarantees. Had the ECB refused to do so (as it had at first dangerously hinted in 2010), the banks holding this public debt would not have been able to sell it. The result would have been a banking crisis and a crisis of public debt fatal for the country in question (and probably leading to its exit from the eurozone).

By accepting very risky securities that might have incurred losses down the line as a loan guarantee, the ECB was able to safeguard the European Union and avoid a financial crisis. But what justified its doing so? This gray area has continued to haunt discussions of the ECB and its actions ever since. In July 2012,

Mario Draghi, who was then chairing the ECB's board of directors, announced that the central bank was "ready to do whatever it takes" to preserve the euro. A few months later, in September, these words were embodied in an institution: the ECB agreed—under certain conditions—to buy, via the markets, the public debt of a member country in a crisis.[5] These potential purchases were called "outright monetary transactions" (OMT). However, they were never implemented.

THE EUROPEAN DEBT CRISIS

With Draghi's proposal for OMT, the central bank's role in the maintenance of European unity, and also in the financing of the welfare state in member countries, was accepted as a matter of fact. But the legal and democratic framework for these principles remained vague. For some observers, the role of insurer that the ECB played created a situation of moral hazard: a country could pursue an irresponsible budgetary policy under the certainty that the central bank would find a way to redeem its debt.

To avoid this moral hazard, the OMT was accompanied by an important conditional clause: the country in crisis had to first call upon the European Stability Mechanism (ESM), a European agency that would assess on what conditions a country could benefit from the aid of the European Commission and, therefore, of the ECB.

At the same time, the ECB was part of the troika (with the International Monetary Fund and the European Commission) seeking to produce an audit of the Greek economic situation and to propose the measures to be imposed on Greece by its creditors. Some of these measures were a clear attack on the welfare state and wrongly imposed fiscal austerity to reduce public debt. As the European Parliament rightly pointed out, the ECB's role within the troika was illegitimate, with a mandate described as "not being clearly defined and lacking in transparency and democratic oversight."[6]

Ultimately, no country asked for the help of OMT, but the ECB was not through with the government's reckoning with public debt. First, the legality of the OMT was contested in the Court of Justice of the EU (CJEU). Then, in 2015, the ECB decided to follow the example of Japan, the United States, and United Kingdom, pursuing a policy of "quantitative easing" (QE) by purchasing massive amounts of public debt.

The difference between QE and OMT is important. OMT is a commitment made by the central bank to buy the public debt of a given country in the event of a crisis and on the condition that budgetary and political reforms be carried out. The purchase of assets in QE makes no distinction between countries and does not impose any conditions. In theory, its goal is not to resolve a public debt crisis but to restart inflation and economic growth. To do so, the central bank begins buying long-term assets in order to cause the long-term interest rate to fall. (The long-term rate is usually higher than the short-term interest rate.)

By causing this long-term rate to decrease, the central bank sought to push businesses and states to make more long-term investments and thus to restart economic growth and (healthy) inflation. The ECB stopped buying Greek debt in 2018, when Greece exited its ESM-supervised program of financial restructuring. Similar conditions remain in the offing if an EU member country is unable to meet its commitments to its other creditors.

In the ECB's vocabulary, it is said that QE makes it possible to restore the "mechanism of transmitting monetary policy," that is, the way in which the ECB's decisions affect the economy, especially prices. For its part, the Court of Justice of the EU has confirmed this interpretation, adding two important qualifications along with it. QE constitutes a monetary policy, not a direct monetary financing of governments, because the purchasing program is not a "certain" preliminary commitment to buy public debt. In fact, QE can be halted or modified at any time. Therefore, a state cannot plan its annual budget by predicting precisely and with certainty the amount of debt that will be bought by the ECB. Second, the CJEU ruled that the purchase of assets must be "proportionate" to the objective.[7] In other words, the central bank must provide theoretical and empirical evidence indicating that QE will have a beneficial effect on the economy, in accordance with the central bank's mandate.

It doesn't take a specialist on monetary policy to understand that QE also has an effect on the possibility of a public debt crisis, as would any intervention that commits the central bank to automatically buying large swaths of public debt. But the COVID-19 pandemic effectively demolished whatever ceiling on central bank debt purchases may have existed before then: Purchases of assets began to rise again with the onset of the pandemic, reaching unimaginable heights (on average, almost 75 percent of the debt issued by European countries, starting with the beginning of the pandemic) and with greater flexibility than previously displayed. The ECB initially promised that purchases of public debt would be made in proportion to the size of the country.[8] This rule remains in force, but its interpretation has become more flexible, and the ECB is authorized to deviate from it to meet the needs of economic and financial stability. The ECB also began buying Greek debt again, without conditions.

Overall, the ECB has made it clear that the purchase of public debt is essential to guaranteeing financial stability, which is in turn essential to avoid excessively harmful consequences in prices and unemployment. This also means that in coming years, the ECB will have to provide further justifications for these purchases, which will in turn require—or perhaps further delay—debate on how these measures relate to states' fiscal policies.

BROKEN TABOOS

Central banks' vast and unprecedented accumulation of public debt between 2008 and 2020 shattered a taboo that was as old as central banks themselves. But it wasn't the only taboo they broke during this period. Even if it was in the news less often than the purchase of public debt, the central banks' granting of long-term loans to banks was undoubtedly an even greater break with respect to these institutions' historical practices. In history, examples of buying public debt are legion, but long-term loans are rarer, and they were generally practiced only during the phase of economic reconstruction after World War II.

The central banks often traditionally disavowed this practice for two reasons. First—and perhaps wrongly—long-term loans were considered inflationary because they led to monetary creation over a longer period. Second, they were seen as investment operations rather than refinancing or injections of liquidity, so they were thus thought to infringe too much on the role of public investment banks. When they were used frequently (mainly during the 1950s–1970s in Europe), it was almost exclusively in operations to refinance these public banks, which themselves specialized in long-term investment.

The launch of long-term loans by the ECB ("long-term refinancing operations," or LTROs, in 2011) and the Bank of England ("funding for lending," then later "term funding scheme") thus represented a major break with the past. The reason: despite the central banks' other loans and securities purchases, which were already substantial, the private banks had not reduced their interest rates enough to drive lending to households. To this end, the central banks therefore decided to offer the banks a guarantee of financing over a long period (up to three years in the case of the ECB) at a low rate of interest.

The insurance offered by long-term loans led the central banks to break another taboo: targeted lending. After the 2008 crisis, the central banks were afraid that the banks would use the security of long-term financing mainly to grant real estate loans to households rather than financing small- and medium-sized businesses. Thus, the ECB's LTRO became the TLTRO (targeted long-term refinancing operation). The term "targeted" here indicates that the banks had to promise that the loans granted by central bank would be used to finance activities defined by that same central bank.

The central bank broke a long-standing taboo by packaging its credit with directions for the credit's use. After World War II, many central banks had developed the habit of announcing that they were granting loans to banks on the condition that those banks use the money to finance precise activities, in particular those that were in accord with the priorities defined by the government. In this way, the central banks participated in the planned economy— the government's industrial or commercial policy. To adopt the terms used in a report issued by the United States Congress documenting this phenomenon on the international level in 1971, the central banks "promote economic and social welfare programs" by "designating certain sectors of the economy that would receive preferred treatment by the central bank."[9]

CREDIT ON CONDITIONS

As financial systems were liberalized and deregulated beginning in the 1980s, the power of monetary policy to set interest rates and act on the business cycle was not questioned, but the economic-planning practices of central banks ended in the United States and wealthy countries in Europe. Where they were once stewards of industrial policies through credit guidance, central banks were now independent, and by the 1990s their retreat from economic planning was an important condition for that independence. Independence was seen as the reward for the central banks' commitments to provide only short-term financing for banks via the market, as opposed to financing one privileged sector or another by means of long-term loans.

The appearance of TLTROs in 2014 thus constituted a rethinking of the liberal doctrine of the central banks that had been established and cemented during the 1990s. However, contrary to what their name suggested, the targeting of these loans was very broad, and the ECB never actually drew up lists of the amounts they agreed conditionally to lend per economic sector. The TLTROs were thus far from the kind of industrial policy that might have been rejected on the principle of free competition—a principle that was written into the European Union treaties and that defined the ECB's mandate. They were instituted with the intent of fixing failures of the market.

But there are *many* failures of the market, and the TLTROs did not fail to provoke lively debates about their use to finance some seemingly defined investments, particularly relating to environmental initiatives.[10] It is part of the ECB's mandate that the central bank is to support the European Union's general policies, which include full employment and protection of the environment. Targeting its loans would be the principal tool for doing so. But is the bank guiding industrial policy when it does so?

These debates become more vigorous as the international context evolves. For example: China has never followed in the footsteps of the European and North American free-market economics of the 1990s, and the country's economy remains, in many regards, planned by the state. China's central bank is accordingly not independent, and its sector-by-sector decisions around credit and financing reflect that orientation. China's increasing political and economic influence forces the European Union to more explicitly define the framework of its monetary policy, including its compatibility with the central bank's independence, by targeting credit toward ends that support the European Union's political and economic goals, *including* environmental goals. Meanwhile the Bank of Japan, another central bank that is legally independent, established a loan program in 2021 that offered preferential rates of interest for banks that financed projects advancing the ecological transition, including renewable energies. The glass case of central bank independence in liberal democracies is quietly cracking.

THE BANKS AND DEMOCRACY

The principle that guided the central banks in breaking these different taboos since 2008 was insurance: The central banks are responsible for providing security for financial actors and for the economy more broadly, and to that end they have spent this century doing what they had to do. But since central banks still operate by lending to the financial sector, it is legitimate to wonder whether the favors paid to private banks during this time can be justified in the name of the common interest—or to safeguarding private interests. Critically, this is not a question that is exclusive to the activities of the central bank but one that must be asked of every organ of the welfare state whose activities are partly based on private intermediaries. Here, the intermediary is the financial sector.

Central banks increasingly protect banks not just from catastrophe but from simple hardship as well. The ECB is special case, as it effectively offered financial compensation to private banks to prevent their profits from being adversely affected by new, complex measures in monetary policy and negative interest rates (the policy of central banks charging fees, in essence, on private banks' deposits in the central bank). But here the ECB was not alone: several other central banks around the world set up a system to limit the potentially damaging effects of monetary policy on banks' profits.

We have seen that the central bank's creation of money for the purpose of buying securities or granting loans is carried out by increasing the banks' reserves (that is, deposits) in the central bank. The central bank remunerates these reserves (i.e., the deposits) at an interest rate that is also an important instrument of its monetary policy: banks navigate the ups and downs of these rates by modulating the interest rates they grant to individuals and businesses on loans or deposits.

Amid consecutive economic crises, the ECB and other central banks lowered this rate as much as it could, to the point that it was negative; a negative rate means that the banks pay when they keep their deposits in the central bank. Negative rates have also led some central banks to fear that private banks' profits would suffer too much, which in turn could hurt the economy.

Since raising all the rates was out of the question (doing so would have had a recessive effect on the economy), a decision was made in 2019 to increase the rate only on the private banks' deposits in the central bank (a "tiering system"). In doing so, central banks adopted measures that sought openly to favor profits of commercial banks, based on a belief that a decline in banks' profits due to the measures of monetary policy would be counterproductive for the economy.

In the European case, the central bank went even further from 2020 to 2022 by allowing the commercial banks to borrow at an interest rate lower than the one at which it was remunerating their deposits: the private banks got to have their cake (higher interest on reserves) and eat it too (lower interest on loans). The difference between these two rates constituted a direct subsidy to the banks, as the central bank pays them more to remunerate their deposits than it asks of them in exchange for a loan.[11] On their own, these individual interventions constitute powerful tools of monetary policy. But taken together and to seemingly opposite ends, they raise the question of the legitimacy of this subsidy: Why not give a subsidy of the same kind to states or individuals?

Notably, there is a final taboo that the ECB has not (yet) overtly violated: risk-taking with its own funds. When the ECB buys corporate debt (bonds), it only buys bonds that are deemed very safe by rating agencies. The risks taken by the ECB are accordingly limited, but they do not change the central bank's commitment to act as an insurer; often the ECB promises to buy these assets from the banks in times of crisis. Other central banks, meanwhile, have not hesitated to operate at greater risk. Principally, these may concern very risky loans to bankrupt institutions (sometimes called the purchase of "toxic assets"). This what the United States Federal Reserve did to save the financial firms AIG and Bear Stearns, in coordination with the Department of the Treasury, in the throes of the 2008 crisis.[12]

The Bank of Japan has taken on even greater risk by purchasing shares in certain companies, as opposed to bonds. The price of shares being much more volatile than that of bonds, shares are considered riskier. As in other domains of monetary policy—in particular, purchases of public debt as a central plank of quantitative easing—Japan has functioned as the canary in the coal mine for central banks operating in crisis. Since 2010, the Bank of Japan has been particularly active in financing real estate, buying shares in the main funds created in 2001 in order to restructure the sector in support of the Japanese government's larger policy goals. This policy broke the central bank taboo around sectoral financing, and since 2011 the Bank of Japan has continued to purchase larger and more diversified set of shares.

For its part, the US Federal Reserve implemented new measures during the pandemic—the Main Street Lending Program— that were equivalent to direct loans to businesses and cities in the United States. In concrete terms, a business that sought to benefit from the measure had to approach a traditional private bank and request a loan from the Fed. This approach ran counter to the principle according to which the central bank refinances only already existing loans: here, loans were granted to businesses in part because the central bank had authorized it. In doing so, the government of the United States made explicit that the state had assumed the risk of the loan. The central bank had operated on behalf of the government in the private sector.

LOANS BETWEEN CENTRAL BANKS

Another crucial element of the central banks' response to the financial crisis of 2008 was international cooperation, which primarily took the form of loans (swap lines) in US dollars. But this cooperation was for the most part asymmetrical: the US central bank, the Fed, became a lender of last resort for entirety of the international system.

A country's power in the international monetary and financial system can be measured by its capacity to come out on top following a crisis that it itself caused. On two occasions, the United States has been a particularly glaring case in point. The first was in 1971, when a monetary crisis provoked by the struggling dollar led to the collapse of the Bretton Woods system, a period in economic history that ultimately and paradoxically left the dollar in its uncontested role as the world's dominant reserve currency. A comparable situation occurred in the financial crisis of 2007–

2008, which had its origin in the US mortgage market. While many predicted the dollar would collapse, the crisis instead provoked a spike in the demand for dollars in order to shore up the liquidity of foreign banks in the international financial markets.

When the crisis of 2008 occurred, many non-US private banks (particularly in Europe and Southeast Asia) were indebted in international markets in dollars, and accordingly they had to repay their creditors in that same currency. But confronted by the panic in the markets, they were no longer able to borrow dollars to reimburse their loans. They then turned to their central banks, which also did not have enough available reserves in dollars. All over the world, central banks asked the Fed for dollars. So the Fed came to the rescue of the private foreign banks by passing dollars through various central banks.[13]

In March 2020, after a brief hiatus due to the COVID-19 pandemic, the Fed resumed making these loans to fourteen foreign central banks. Other central banks also made international loans in response to demand for their currencies. The ECB lent to the central banks of Eastern Europe (outside the eurozone), where the banks were indebted in euros.[14]

These loans, known as "swap lines," surely played an important role in avoiding a still more massive financial crisis in the midst of COVID-19. And that was just how the central banks justified them. The arguments advanced were similar to those that were deployed to justify quantitative easing and other new measures that had been undertaken to confront twenty-first-century crises: A central bank has to use all the tools available to it in order to guarantee financial stability, which is the necessary prerequisite for its ability to achieve its monetary policy goals (targeting inflation, employment). Had the Japanese and European banks been forced to withdraw completely from the US market, the impact on the United States, too, would have been significant, even devastating.

But it cannot be denied that this kind of operation also has diplomatic and political stakes. The ECB granted loans (swap lines) to the central banks of Sweden and Denmark, but initially refused to do so for Poland and Hungary in 2009, even though the risk of financial contagion—particularly between these countries and Austria—was proven. It took several months for the ECB to accept that it was diplomatically and economically unjustified to differentiate between European countries in this way.[15]

Swap lines between central banks are not new. In the nineteenth century, the Bank of France made this type of loan to the Bank of England, on several occasions, when the latter was going through a crisis.[16] It was not a matter of altruism, but rather to allow the Bank of England to lend to British banks—and, for France, to avoid extending the negative impact of the crisis on the French financial system.

This was an early, isolated case. It was not until the 1960s that loans between central banks became systematic over a period of more than a decade, first in support of the Bretton Woods international monetary system, then later to support the liberalization of the international capital markets. At that time, it was already a privilege enjoyed by rich countries that could get around the International Monetary Fund and its conditional loans. But contrary to their use in 2008, these earlier swap-line loans had as their goal maintaining the dollar's stability. They were also part of a larger, multilateral framework by a group of central banks at the Bank for International Settlements (BIS).

Today, that kind of multilateral framework is lacking, and these loans between central banks reflect solely the asymmetry of the international system: in the event of a crisis, some countries have to request aid from the central bank of the country issuing international reserves; that is, mainly, the United States. It is because of this asymmetry that the European Union has begun to discuss the appropriateness of reducing the dependence of its banks on the dollar in financial markets. But reducing this dependence means promoting the euro as an international reserve currency—and with that role, lending to foreign central banks in case of a crisis.

Whereas the bilateral loans made by the Fed and the ECB arose from the will to support financial markets functioning in dollars and euros, China's central bank (the People's Bank of China, or PBoC) has instituted loans that function similarly but for different reasons. The PBoC has signed swap lines with thirty-nine countries, twenty-eight of them emerging markets—at least twice as many partners as the United States. The swap lines in the Chinese currency, the renminbi (RMB), encourage the currency's use in cross-border payments, and they are designed to finance commercial credit and short-term public debt. They differ from those of the Fed, which were designed to respond to foreign banks' needs for financing in dollars. China's goal is therefore not to save a financial system based on its currency but to promote the use of its currency in international commercial trade and loans, especially in emerging economies.[17]

The amounts actually borrowed through these swap lines remain secret, but China is potentially making $580 billion available. The outstanding bilateral loan amount from the Fed's swap lines has reached $450 billion, although more could be borrowed in accordance with the agreements currently in place. During the COVID-19 crisis in 2020, the amount that could be borrowed through these bilateral loans was twice as much as could be borrowed from the International Monetary Fund.[18] Before the 2008 crisis, the IMF's loans dominated most of the liquid assets made available to countries by states or international organizations. The new monetary diplomacy is thus based on the predominance of bilateral loans and the marginalization of the multilateral framework inherited from World War II.[19] Furthermore, this swap-line proliferation has been accompanied by an increase of other financing networks, including those between central banks grouped within frameworks of regional accords—like the Chiang Mai Initiative, a multilateral currency swap arrangement among ten countries in Southeast Asia. In 2020, the total of the loans resulting from these regional accords approached $1,200 billion—a sum close to the total of bilateral loans between central banks.

Loans between central banks thus raise the question of who is authorized to make such financial decisions, which carry major geopolitical consequences. In Europe, it appears to be the ECB that is primarily charged with the decision-making, even though exchange rate policy is normally the responsibility of the Council of the European Union. The ECB also offers advantageous credit conditions to countries in the process of monetary integration into the eurozone, like Croatia and Bulgaria.[20] This choice is not a problem in itself, but it deserves to be more clearly justified and founded in law, supported, for example, by a decision of the European Parliament or the Council. In the case of Europe and the United States—even if the sums at stake are very different—the democratic question is the same: Are loans made to foreign central banks through swap lines comparable to the traditional operations of the central bank (open-market purchase of foreign securities for foreign exchange operations) or to direct loans made outside the market? To put the question a different way: Are these bilateral loans part of foreign policy or do they simply facilitate the execution of monetary policy by limiting the financial risks? In the case of the United States, following stormy debates in Congress, the question that arose was whether the Fed's loans to foreign central banks should be treated as open-market operations (in which case they are subject to section 14 of the Federal Reserve Act, requiring approval of any negotiations with foreign banks by the Fed's board of governors) or whether their legal treatment should instead draw on section 13(3), which permits the Fed to lend directly to particular institutions in the event of financial risk but in agreement with the Treasury.[21] A shift from section 14 to section 13(3) would thus imply the reintegration of bilateral loans into the foreign policy of the US government. These parliamentary and juridical debates, which are certainly technical, show how the new geopolitical outgrowths of monetary policy require a sturdy democratic institutional framework—and how the existence of such a framework remains elusive.

OVERSEEING FINANCIAL FLOWS

Bilateral loans between central banks form a new kind of monetary geopolitics. Even if international financial integration remains high and, on the whole, little hindered, it is also increasingly subject to sovereigntist demands or strategic alliances between countries. The sanctions imposed on Russia following its invasion of Ukraine in 2022 are another clear example of the connection between international financial architecture and geopolitics. The sanctions were of unprecedented breadth, including the freeze of Russia's exchange reserves and the suspension of the Bank of Russia from the Bank for International Settlements. But it was neither the first nor the only recent example of sanctions executed through the international financial system; the United States had previously imposed similar measures on Iran and Venezuela. The sanctions came after Russia's years-long accumulation of exchange reserves, an effort intended to ensure the country's autonomy. Those assets were largely frozen by the foreign sanctions.

Beyond open conflicts and sanctions, states' broader control of international financial flows has been reinstated—a reversal from the financial liberalization of the 1980s and 1990s. The doctrine of these earlier decades concerning the international financial architecture—defended in particular in Europe, the United States, and the IMF—gave priority to freedom of capital and flexible exchange rates. Although the financial crises at the end of the 1990s, most notably in Asia, along with the harsh criticism of financial liberalization, are what motivated this change, it was only after the financial crisis of 2008 that the doctrine of the IMF and other national and international organizations began to evolve. This evolution can be characterized principally as a change of position not only with regard to capital controls—regulatory attempts to limit the flow of foreign capital—but also to state interventions that limited the volatility of their exchange rates.

Along with financial crises and widespread criticism directed at financial liberalization, two political developments further fueled the move to reestablish the legitimacy of capital controls. First was the emergence of China, which embodied a new economic model centered on state control and financial restraints; second, a renewal of economic theories that gave intellectual credence to the role of capital controls. Both the renewed academic literature and the IMF narrative justified capital controls and exchange rate interventions in the name of "prudential" oversight—that is, in the name of financial stability.[22] The main argument here is that international financial flows are determined not merely by the intrinsic characteristics of countries but also by the vagaries of international liquidity, including a global financial cycle that can move a country's interest rate and exchange rate in an undesirable way. More generally, the recent justification of capital controls has been strongly influenced by the realization that the monetary policy of the United States influences financial conditions and capital flows in all other countries, even those that have a flexible exchange rate, and not always for the better.[23]

The divergences between the policies of central banks played an important role in the development of this kind of argument. In September 2010, the Brazilian minister of finance, Guido Mantega, provoked a stir in the normally hushed world of international monetary relations by accusing the United States of waging a currency war. According to Mantega, the Fed's low interest rates were part of an attempt to drive down the American exchange rate to favor exports and to provoke short-term inflows of capital in emerging countries. This would be a potential source of financial stability for the United States, but an albatross for the emerging countries when interest rates increased later on.

The new prudential justification of capital controls was thus founded on observance of the imperfections of international financial markets and their consequences for financial instability. It differs from the idea that capital controls can be useful complements to a national industrial policy seeking to develop certain sectors, or that interventions in exchange rates can help maintain undervalued exchange rates in order to facilitate exports. These other justifications for capital controls managed to prevail at earlier moments in history, and they are still harbored by some emerging countries. While the more recent theoretical justification of capital controls has undeniably had effects on the discourse of international organizations and different countries, it nonetheless does not reflect how capital controls are actually used. The majority of countries that use these controls maintain them over the long term, often with internal economic policy goals.[24]

The sea change of ideas and narratives in monetary policy therefore reflects political changes rather imperfectly. It seems that there is a loose international agreement that capital controls should no longer be regarded as undignified tools. But even this modest claim comes with strong qualifications. The IMF's position essentially justifies capital controls as a hedge against a global financial cycle and refuses to take into account the different objectives of domestic policies.[25] Meanwhile countries like China speak in terms like "macroprudential" to justify the implementation of capital controls to preserve financial stability, but in practice they defend a much broader view of capital controls, steered by administrative decisions that evaluate investments based on the domestic objectives of credit or monetary policy.[26]

Even if there are notable differences in the arguments defending capital controls, it is undeniable that they have regained their legitimacy and use. It is no longer possible to think about the policy of the central banks without thinking about controls on international financial flows, either because some central banks administer these controls themselves (reserve ratios on foreign assets in China, for example), or because the central banks' policies directly interact with these controls, likely in their own countries and abroad.

THE THREAT OF DIGITAL CURRENCIES

Since shortly after the 2008 financial crisis, new forms of money have been in the headlines for one reason or another. Cryptocurrencies, or digital currencies (the best-known of which is Bitcoin), are part of a larger and no doubt irreversible movement: a move away from payments made with coins and bills in favor instead of payment by digital means (credit cards, apps, online transfers between accounts, etc.).

Most digital means of payment are not, however, new forms of currency. They are not even the virtual equivalents of coins and bills: they are not anonymous, not accepted everywhere, they typically require a bank account, and they frequently involve transaction costs (paid to the bank or financial institution that handles the payment). Cryptocurrencies, on the contrary, seek to have the same privacy properties as bank bills but in a dematerialized form. They explicitly aim to get around banking systems and traditional means of payment that track movements of money between people and accounts.

The first cryptocurrencies that appeared were private—that is, they had no connection with states. Their emergence produced major consequences for public authorities and the central banks. First, they raised a problem of regulation—the impossibility of policing fraudulent uses of these currencies, over which the state had little control. Second, private cryptocurrencies constituted a potential danger to financial stability, the functioning of monetary policy, and the protection of citizens' savings.

If states and central banks no longer oversee their currency, it will no longer be possible for them to act on macroeconomic fluctuations (the core objective of monetary policy) or to save the banking and financial system in the event of a crisis (the role of lender of last resort). Moreover, for the state, accepting the emergence of a private currency is tantamount to abandoning its role as protector of the value of the money held by citizens—that is, to letting citizens suffer potentially significant losses when the value of private currencies fluctuates or crashes.

Thus, the stakes for states and central banks are clear: They have to issue their own cryptocurrencies to address the different threats that hang over their sovereignty and the financial protection of their citizens. The first threat is constituted by private digital currencies, such as Bitcoin, or by other commercial enterprises that might become dominant for transactions and storing value. The second is the disappearance of the currency in circulation (anonymous, transparent, cost-free, and accessible to everyone) and its replacement by digital means of payment that are subject to the financial and commercial conditions of the companies that manage them. A digital currency issued by a central bank should therefore be fully substitutable for cash (bills and coins) and, like the bills and coins, its existence should not be dependent on commercial banks.

In spite of their number and diversity (today, there are several thousand of them, easily accessible on the internet), private cryptocurrencies have two points in common: they are entirely digital and they are not issued by a state (that is, by a central bank). And unlike bills and coins, which offer citizens confidence and reliability based on their material appearance, a cryptocurrency confers its authenticity based on an algorithmic ledger, the blockchain, which validates both the creation and transaction of these currencies, and thus prevents piracy or computer falsification.

Consumer confidence in this system is not based on any commitments from the central bank. Instead, to guarantee long-term confidence, the total quantity of Bitcoin created is limited by the original algorithm. The closer the limit, the more computing power is needed to verify the transactions. The result is a destructive system in which, to guarantee confidence in this currency, the production of Bitcoin becomes more and more energy-consuming (via computers' calculation time).

Stability can also be assumed thanks to the belief in the self-regulation of a decentralized market (i.e., one separate from the state) or by the existence of a tightly knit community coming to agreement in order to resolve the problems of piracy or price volatility. In the case of Bitcoin, this has led to occasional surges of prices driven by a purely speculative demand. It has also led to spectacular crashes based on the community- and personality-driven regulation of cryptocurrencies broadly, as with the FTX crash in 2022. Bitcoin is little used *qua* money for payments but rather as an asset that might produce future profits.

Other cryptocurrencies (called "stablecoins") seek to win confidence by indexing their value to a set of existing secure currencies. This was the case with Diem, the currency that Facebook proposed but finally abandoned: a foundation manages the currency and holds in reserve the equivalent of Diems in governmental securities or in currency. This guarantees the convertibility (and thus the exchange rate) of this currency. Hence the goal—with a view to private profits connected with an increase in commercial transactions—is to lean on existing state-issued currencies in order to profit from the confidence they inspire. But without regulation, nothing can guarantee users that the business that issues this money really has sufficient reserves. And once they are regulated, the companies that issue stablecoins are not so different from commercial banks proposing new payment functionalities or loans with advance technologies.

A CENTRAL BANK DIGITAL CURRENCY?

It is therefore essential that a central bank issue a digital currency in order to keep monetary transactions from being increasingly carried out through private currencies. One can imagine, not improbably, that the majority of individuals could someday soon use mainly Facebook's or Amazon's currencies to make purchases online (or even going so far as to ask their employer to pay their salaries in these currencies—especially as tech companies become larger employers). That would create significant problems of sovereignty.

First, there would be a submission to the terms of the contracts signed by these private operators, who would in turn be able to decide to modify the currency's exchange rate, its sphere of use (and thus its convertibility), or the policy concerning the data associated with transactions. In its traditional role, the state would no longer be able to lower interest rates or to create money to counter an economic or financial crisis.

Countering the power of private currencies is therefore a duty of states. But the creation of a digital currency by a central bank also raises important questions on the level of democracy, whether regarding the anonymity of transactions or the new financial role that such a technology offers the central bank. Whatever the technology adopted for these transactions, an official digital currency implies that every citizen has an account at the central bank that serves as his "wallet." As institutions that liaise with states and private banks but not with individual citizens, this would be unprecedented territory for central banks.

Most economists and central bankers currently think that this option of individual central bank accounts, which bypasses private banks and guarantee the anonymity of transactions, is the only one that truly corresponds to the nature of a public (i.e., official) digital currency and provides a genuine digital equivalent to paper money. Others propose to follow the Chinese model, in which citizens have a digital wallet in a commercial bank that deposits the same amount of reserves in an account at the central bank (and transmits all the information concerning the related transactions). If that came to wholly replace coins and bills, there would be a significant threat to the anonymity of transactions.[27]

Anonymity is needed not solely to carry out fraudulent operations; it is also required for the inherently private uses of the currency and the moral value that is associated with them. Paradoxically, the loss of anonymity could even damage confidence in the official currency and lead individuals to use other forms of money.[28] For these reasons, no doubt, the hypothetical creation of a digital currency in Europe would not lead to an immediate disappearance of cash, as some statements made by the ECB have suggested.[29]

These debates are far from over, especially since, if a digital currency is created that cannot be redeemed for cash (even if it is a stablecoin, that is, a digital euro entirely indexed to the original euro), then it will technically be a different currency. The decision to create it will therefore not be for the central bank alone to make. A parliamentary or congressional debate—or in the European case, an intergovernmental debate—will be necessary.

The creation of a digital currency issued by the central bank also implies reflection on the central bank's role within the financial system. If the digital currency takes the form of a traditional bank account, as in China (with the digital yuan), commercial banks become mere operators of the central bank, and, in a certain way, operators of a public service. Even if commercial banks are already highly regulated, it can be asked whether their role as operators of a public service should not lead the state to set new conditions for their governance, the remuneration of their employees and managers, or other matters.

And if a digital currency is based on deposits in the central bank, then part of the traditional role of commercial banks will disappear. The sums involved do not allow us to think that commercial banks would suffer enormously from the curtailment of this activity.[30] But the existence of accounts at the central bank could nonetheless constitute a threat to financial stability. As the 2023 collapse of Silicon Valley Bank in the United States demonstrated, individuals who fear a possible bankruptcy of their bank will often decide to withdraw all their deposits and put them elsewhere—that, potentially, could include a wallet at the central bank with digital money. If all individuals opened an account at the central bank in order to make their everyday payments, the organization of the banking system would be thrown into utter confusion. To avoid such confusion and risk to financial stability, economists have proposed that a cap be placed on the central bank's digital currency account or wallet.[31] For a large portion of the population (those whose incomes are too small to allow them to save; often about a third of the population in wealthy economies), that may entail depositing all salaries and welfare benefits in the account at the central bank. This situation is far from unimaginable, and one might even think that, properly organized, it might benefit the least advantaged, notably by decreasing the costs of account maintenance, that is, by making the use of the currency completely free. The alternative—on the model developed in China—would be to strengthen the public-private partnership between the central bank and the commercial banks. The latter would maintain an account in digital money for their customers that was different from a classic deposit account, and they would deposit the equivalent amount in the central bank. In a democracy, this solution can be envisaged only if the central bank can set strict conditions for the banks to guarantee universal access at no cost and the anonymity of monetary transactions. Access to the currency is a right that cannot be made conditional on the acceptance of a service and a commercial contract.

DIGITAL MONETARY POLICY

For all its potential for foundational disruption, digital currency issued by the central bank could equally provide new tools for monetary policy, since the state would have direct control over the money held by individuals—a tool that could be used to steer and monitor the economy.[32]

Two possibilities can be envisaged: First, the central bank could remunerate individuals' deposits through interest rates. A high interest rate could make it possible to fight inflation; a negative interest rate could compel individuals to use this money to buy things, as some economists advocate.

Is that a legitimate monetary policy, or would negative interest rates on liquid currency (that is, a destruction of the currency by the central bank) violate the moral pact between the state and its citizens? For economists, negative rates are equivalent to inflation, because they diminish—in different ways—the real value of the currency. But this argument reduces the monetary question to a purely technical question and ignores the moral aspect, which is nonetheless essential for the confidence that is at the foundation of the currency.

Another instrument of monetary policy whose use would be facilitated by a central digital currency is "helicopter money"—that is, direct transfers of money to individuals. To do so, in fact, it would suffice for the central bank to credit individuals' accounts, in the same way as the US government did in March 2020, with the Coronavirus Aid, Relief, and Economic Security Act (CARES Act). We will discuss this option in the last chapter. Some commentators maintain that paying out money without receiving something in return breaks a moral taboo on treating money as worthless. This, too, is a question that must be opened to democratic debate.

A final issue must be mentioned here, especially since, alongside questions of feasibility and precedent raised by digital currency, it has not received much attention, even in the central banks' numerous publications on the subject. To put it plainly: What would the central bank do with all the money deposited by private individuals? If digital money is truly a substitute for fiduciary money (cash), digital money would seemingly merely replace cash on the central bank's balance sheet.

But as we have seen, an authentic central bank currency would come to replace part of the most liquid bank deposits that currently serve as the basis for payments by the majority of the population. By doing so, it would play a public service role and guarantee everyone equal access to digital means of payment. It is difficult to predict how individuals would allocate their finances in this case, but it is not implausible that, for people whose savings are small and consist of a few hundred or a few thousand dollars in their current account, the central bank's account would become their main deposit account. (Putting a ceiling on the account at the central bank would limit, but not entirely prevent, that outcome.) Then the question of the central bank's investment—what it does with the deposits from the general public—will necessarily arise. Where and how should these liquid savings, no matter how small they might be compared with total savings, be invested? Would that make possible a new channel for financing the public debt and, if so, how could it be institutionalized? In countries like France, where there are already regulated liquid savings accounts to finance social housing ("livret A"), should the central bank be in charge of these savings, or should they be entrusted to the public development banks that presently manage them? Would an independent structure have to be created to handle these assets, on the model of the investment fund managed by Norway's central bank or on the model of France's Caisse des dépôts?

The debate about digital currencies arrives at a critical moment for central banks. It is clear that any digital currency issued by central banks would serve to recast not only the relationship between the central bank and the state, but also the relationship between the central bank and the general public. With added considerations such as the ecological transition, this digital outgrowth of public banking constitutes a test, in every sense, of what ends the central bank aims to serve.

Central Banks Everywhere

In economists' ideal world, central banks all function more or less in the same way. At the end of the nineteenth century, their operations had to follow the principles of the gold standard and thus respect what Maynard Keynes called the "rules of the game": increasing interest rates when gold left the country in order to attract foreign capital and stabilize the exchange rate. At the end of the twentieth century, gold no longer being the guide of monetary policy, central banks decided to follow an inflation target instead, increasing their interest rates when the actual rate of inflation exceeded the inflation target. In this framework, the exchange rate has to fluctuate freely in relation to the differences in countries' rates of inflation. At the end of the twentieth century, as at the end of the nineteenth, these models of central bank policy were established at a time of accelerating financial globalization. They were consistent with the notion that liberal globalization was going to establish a shared model for organizing financial systems and monetary policy in all countries.[1]

These models only partly reflect reality. In both historical examples, it is undeniable that financial globalization had strong effects in bringing the practices of the various central banks closer together. It is also undeniable that the manipulation of interest rates aimed at achieving the periods' main stated objectives: the stability of the exchange rate and the gold reserves during the two decades that preceded the beginning of World War I, and the inflation target in the two decades preceding the 2008 financial crisis. But such generalizations tend to blind us to the persistence of very different practices and objectives among central banks. The differences persist because these institutions evolve in their own political contexts and financial systems, each of which has its own peculiarities and history. It is in the details of financial operations—interactions with other actions carried out by the state and the interpretation of laws governing central banks— that the political stakes of monetary management are to be found. Even if the central banks seem to change their interest rates for the same reasons, the ways in which they lend to financial institutions, supervise the banks, interact with the government, and are overseen by the parliament can still differ greatly.[2]

The differences between central banks reappeared clearly after the 2008 crisis, when they had to struggle to support, at arm's length, failing financial systems and play an essential role in maintaining the stability of economies, even of political systems. When their insurance function and providential role returned to center stage, their connection with national characteristics of states and financial systems became clearer. This as much concerns direct loans to banks (and sometimes even to businesses) as it does the purchase of public debt or macroprudential policy. These circumstances also made it possible to see that the central banks were in fact inserting themselves into a general credit policy, even if, depending on the country, that policy was more or less acknowledged as interventionist.

By resituating the central banks in the context of the welfare state and their national banking system, the succession of crises from 2008 to 2022 (financial crises, public debt crises in certain countries, and then the pandemic) has thus increased their differences, just as it did in the middle of the twentieth century, from the 1930s to the 1980s. Even if the reality is that there has never been a single model for central banks, including during the first phase of globalization before 1914, the central banks' practices diverge all the more when their monetary policies interact with their local state policies. The central banks have therefore rediscovered the "variety of capitalisms" level of diversity that has long characterized the various welfare states.[3]

The impossibility of a single model for the central bank is due not only to the succession of economic and financial crises that have reinforced national particularities and national credit policies. The emergence of China has provided a countermodel, with less financial liberalization and greater integration of the central banks into credit policy. This model obviously does not display democratic characteristics, and the discussion of the legitimacy of the country's credit policy is typically reduced to the will of the Communist Party. But the capital controls imposed by China in order to maintain its financial independence and its aid to foreign economic development based on bilateral loans (including alternatives to those of international institutions) appeal to countries that became skeptical of liberal globalization in the course of the 1990s. In addition, through a rapid commitment to putting credit policy (including the central bank) in the service of the battle against climate change, China has for the first time appeared as a leading country within the international community of central banks. The first report of the Network of Central Banks and Supervisors for Greening the Financial System, or NGFS, in 2018 announced its character: "Among NGFS Members, so far only one Central Bank, the People's Bank of China, has a dedicated policy to promote green finance via monetary policy."[4] As in the case of digital currency, China rapidly made choices that the central banks in democratic countries know are inevitable but have been slow to make. It constitutes a major challenge to liberal regimes, which are thereby pushed to reinvent a credit policy *and* to make sure that this policy retains democratic characteristics.

This chapter stresses the important differences that exist today between individual central banks' policies as well as the contexts for their actions. It does not claim to be exhaustive; rather, it is based on a few examples (mainly the eurozone, the United States, and China) that allow us to emphasize the diversity of the models and the stakes involved. We shall see that a comparative perspective tends to soften, or at least relativize, the idea that the independence of the central bank has a fixed definition. In addition to the diversity of their financial operations, which was emphasized in the preceding chapter, and of their macroeconomic objectives, central banks also play very different roles in the supervision of banking, financial stability, and exchange rate policy. The interaction of their actions with other components of states' credit policy, which has specific contours depending on the countries and the periods concerned, also demonstrates the impossibility of thinking about monetary policy in isolation.

THE CENTRAL BANK AND THE SOVEREIGN: WHAT KIND OF INDEPENDENCE?

If we had to find common threads—today and historically—in the laws that regulate the activities of central banks, one would be that the laws all define, with relative clarity, the financial instruments (i.e., the types of loans) that central banks can use to make monetary policy and guarantee financial stability. The difference, and the challenge, is that financial stability and the objectives of monetary policy are rarely defined in central bank laws. When they are, their legal status and boundaries differ from one country to another. For example, today most central banks emphasize price stability as an imperative, but the inflation target is not defined by law. In other words, the law may require central banks to set targets for inflation, but the same law says nothing about the rate of inflation that the central bank should consider acceptable.[5] In the United States and in the eurozone, central banks are not even required to announce their inflation target, let alone the weight to be applied to other goals (limiting unemployment in the United States; support for general policies in the case of the eurozone). In other countries, the inflation target must, by law, be determined by the government (as in the United Kingdom) or by an agreement between the government and the central bank (New Zealand).

About half of the world's central banks have objectives other than price stability written into their governing statute.[6] This multitude of objectives, along with the impossibility of fully defining them or explaining them in legal terms, is not for a lack of thought or care. The vagueness that surrounds central banks' expressed goals and powers is rooted in a universal tension: on the one hand, a central bank's independence cannot be complete or total; and on the other hand, it is essential to leave the central bank a margin of interpretation and flexibility so that it can act at its discretion when confronted by uncertain or unexpected circumstances.[7] Accordingly, the central bank's independence has a rather limited meaning—even if it is still significant: it retains the power to say no to a government that asks the central bank to take actions that it would consider contrary to its principal missions as defined by the (purposefully vague) law. It is through such refusals that the independence of the central bank is defined and maintained. Even when the central bank's actions are constrained by the financial tools that the laws have put at its disposal, the space for interpretation remains broad and includes, as we have seen, the determination of objectives.

Laws differ from one country to the next. Practices differ even more, especially since the laws organizing the central banks' actions are subject to diverse interpretations. For example, the Chinese central bank is today more independent than those in many democracies according to legal criteria, but certainly not in practice.[8] These practices reflect national traditions, but they are also very sensitive to personalities. In that regard, the case of the United States in the 1970s is often cited as an example. In 1970, Richard Nixon appointed Arthur Burns as head of the country's central bank. Burns, who had earlier been the president's economic advisor, was the author of influential works on economic cycles and an active member of the Republican Party in the 1950s. He was opposed to Keynesianism, and his works on cycles had caught the attention of Milton Friedman and his disciples. However, the personal and ideological closeness between Burns and Nixon led to the Fed chairman's complete submission to the president's orders, including explicit pressures that drew no opposition. From a strictly legal point of view, the Fed remained no less independent than it is today. Yet all the while, Nixon had managed to enact a law, the Credit Control Act of 1969, that afforded him the power to use banking regulation to limit credit (in particular, consumer credit) in order to fight inflation. In this way, he was copying, albeit on a smaller scale, measures that had been applied in other countries at the behest of the central bank, or through an agreement between the central bank and the government. In the United States, Nixon did it himself. This example provides a good illustration of how deeply the political relationship between the central bank and the government can change without modifying the law, merely because of personality or political convergences between governments and central banks.

Open conflicts between governments and independent central banks are rare. In Germany, the central bank was formally independent during the hyperinflation of 1922 and 1923, and it remained so when a massive financing of the public debt was put in place in 1933, using bonds issued by the MEFO (Metallurgical Research Society, a shell company composed of German manufacturers whose primary customer was the Nazi German government). Not until 1939 did members of the central bank's board of directors resign to protest Adolf Hitler's inflationist policy. The disinflation policies in the United States and then in other countries in the early 1980s were made with the support of governments. In 2021, the president of the German central bank chose to resign following a change in the parliamentary majority, citing an anticipation of disagreements with the new government and a preference for avoiding nonproductive conflict.

However, there are few examples of central banks declaring their opposition to a government policy, to the point of depriving the policy of its legitimacy. In France, in 1952—a period many people wrongly associate with the central banks' lack of independence—the governor of the Banque de France harshly criticized the government's inflationary policies and announced that he would refuse to lend to the central bank under these conditions; obviously, the central bank had no direct control over the government, and his threat was limited to inflation. But his speech received enough support among members of the parliament to allow them to demand and obtain a change of government.

The practice of independence is thus contextual, and it depends above all on the strength or weakness of the government in place alongside the central bank. In the 1950s, when France's central bank asserted itself so boldly, the government was, not coincidentally, also weak and unstable. In the European Union today, the absence of a shared fiscal policy puts an enormous burden on the central bank, which has to navigate the mixed bag of governments and policies among EU member states. But the power of the European Central Bank to criticize governments—even when these criticisms have no direct connection with the objective of price stability—speaks as much to the lack of common European fiscal policy as it does to the power of the ECB. In the eurozone, the ECB's independence did not prevent the bank from participating in the troika in Greece, nor did it prevent the ECB from sending a letter to the Italian prime minister, Silvio Berlusconi, in 2011. This letter, which was signed by ECB governor Jean-Claude Trichet and endorsed by Mario Draghi, the governor of the Bank of Italy, drew up a list of "indispensable measures" that the government should take—ranging from the privatization of public services to the reduction of government officials' salaries, as well as a consti-tutional reform of taxation and the abolition of regional adminis-trative divisions. These positions clearly went far beyond the role assigned to the central bank by legal authorities. For very different reasons, other central banks appeared to be stronger and more sta-ble than their governments during the 2010s: in the United States, because of the political uncertainty caused by Barack Obama's lack of a majority in Congress, then later by Donald Trump's erratic style of government; in the United Kingdom, during the process of Brexit. In Japan, on the contrary, the stability and strength of Shinzo Abe's government between 2012 and 2020 gave the impres-sion of a strong coordination between fiscal policy and monetary policy, guided principally by the former.

Finally, the central banks of these different countries estab-lished programs of quantitative easing (the purchase of public debt) that were relatively similar but had been advanced for seem-ingly different political reasons. The consequences and political debates accompanying their shared monetary actions were also very different. In Europe, attention has focused on the legality of buying public debt and the fiscal rules to be respected by differ-ent countries. It has also been litigious, with several complaints addressed to the European Union Court of Justice, due to the relevance to the ongoing construction of Europe. In the United Kingdom and the United States, the debate centers more squarely on the social and economic consequences of asset purchases by the central bank, notably by raising the question of the alternatives to these policies, whether they involve budgetary expansion or possible direct monetary transfers made by the central bank ("quantitative easing for the people" or "helicopter money"). It was all the more possible because the financial, political, and juridical links between the central bank and the Treasury are in fact much stronger in these two countries.[9] In the United Kingdom, the policy of quantitative easing has led to the creation of a special fund—managed by the Bank of England—that diverts profits directly to the Treasury, and the terms of risk management have been made the object of an agreement between the bank and the Treasury. In the United States, a large part of the central bank's policy during the pandemic was carried out with the legal agreement (and fiscal backing in case of losses) of the Department of the Treasury. The policy of "helicopter money" was finally set up by means of checks paid by the Treasury to individuals while the central bank bought public debt. The debates on the inegalitarian consequences of quantitative easing appeared relatively later in Europe. There, the new doctrine of direct monetary financing of the budgetary deficit (modern monetary theory) also was less influential than in the United States for the simple reason that there was no significant common federal budget. On the contrary, because of the structuring role of European budgetary rules and the fear of a new crisis of public debts repeating the crisis of 2012, some European economists have discussed a possible cancellation of the public debt held by the European Central Bank.[10]

The policies of the central banks and the debates that accompany these policies were thus re-localized even as the banks' role became financially greater and more visible. The institutional structure of the state, the particulars of the financial systems, the stability of the governments, and the careers and personalities of the central bankers have shaped monetary policies and their justification in very different ways, depending on the country. One might be tempted to attribute this resurgence of national differences to inroads on the central banks' independence—or perhaps the attempts at takeover by governments seeking to finance themselves at low cost. But as the political scientist Christopher Adolph has emphasized, it may be because the central banks have independent status by law that their policies can vary greatly, along with the personalities of their leaders. These leaders have more power because they are not subject to recall and have the ability to oppose governments—which potentially increases the singular freedom of interpretation of their objectives while also rendering them more vulnerable to the play of influence in the financial or political spheres.[11] Adolph's analysis of central bankers in the United States shows the extent to which their professional trajectories influence the positions they take—in essence, how exquisitely monetary policy is stamped by the perspective and career of its creators. Similar conclusions have been drawn by recent studies in economics, which shed light on the influence exercised on monetary policies by the organizational culture of central banks and the singular career trajectories of their leaders. This is nothing new. In the 1950s and 1960s, governors of the central bank who had had longer experience with the gold standard prior to World War II were less inclined to abandon gold (as a guarantee of the value of the currency) after the war.[12] The institutional and personal history of the gold standard weighed on the shoulders of the central bankers at the very time that the postwar Bretton Woods system was supposed to break the connections between gold and monetary policy. Then as now, practice differs from the law, and is strongly influenced by the identity of those in charge.

SYSTEMS OF CENTRAL BANKS

The United States and the eurozone share one monetary peculiarity:[13] in both settings, monetary policy is shaped and applied by a central bank *system*, not by a central bank. This structure, the result of historical political compromises in both jurisdictions, leads to great complexity in the legal articulation of their central banks' structures and proceedings.[14] Neither the Federal Reserve System itself nor the European System of Central Banks are legal entities. The Board of Governors of the Federal Reserve System and the ECB are legal entities, and so are the twelve regional banks (in the case of the US Federal Reserve) and twenty national central banks in the eurozone. Through this baroque construction, both systems produce a gap between the site of decision-making and the site of democratic responsibility. In the United States, the Board of Governors is responsible for providing reports and accountability to Congress, but decisions regarding monetary policy are made in the Federal Open Market Committee (FOMC), which also includes five directors of the regional Federal Reserve banks. In Europe, the executive board of the ECB reports to the European Parliament, but the governors of the national central banks have seats on the governing council of the ECB, which takes monetary policy decisions. These governors do not serve as representatives of their countries, because the ECB is not an intergovernmental structure (which explains why a system of voting by rotation is possible). They are responsible to their own national parliament for the actions conducted at the national level by each central bank but not for their votes at the European level.

In both cases, organization as a system can be characterized as beneficial because it contributes to the independence and balance of perspectives by increasing the political and professional diversity of decision-makers. It is an approach to governance loosely equivalent to the designation of ex officio members—people who are not named by a federal executive but named as a form of political representation (regional, in this case) that does not depend on the executive or legislative powers. This type of representation may be completely legitimate; it may also be the case that, considering the relationship between the Federal Reserve's Board of Governors and Congress, it in no way diminishes Congress's ability to express its opinion on the decisions made by the central bank. But the federal structure and the presence of regional representatives on the decision-making council *do* play a major role in the political debate—both internal, for decision-making, and external, with regard to the general public. In the United States, as in the euro-zone, the most divergent points of view are thus often represented by individuals who are neither appointed by the federal executive authority nor confirmed by Congress. Moreover, in public debate, they represent well-identified points of view and political traditions. In the United States, the presidents of the regional Federal Reserve banks in St. Louis, Kansas City, or Dallas traditionally adopt points of view that are more anti-inflationary and more favorable to the market than do their colleagues on the East and West coasts, while in Europe, Germany usually defends a stricter view regarding inflation and the purchase of public debt. The presence of members not named by the federal executive power is thus very important in making decisions concerning monetary policy in the United States and in Europe, and it undoubtedly encourages a diversity of points of view and political independence. But the status of these members remains vague and is often reluctantly accepted in terms of responsibility and democratic legitimacy.

This vagueness is even stronger in the United States because the regional banks have private stockholders:[15] the commercial banks operating in each district. These stockholders elect representatives from the private banks as well as representatives from the "public" (economic activities that do not involve banking—frequently executives from large industries), all of whom sit on each regional bank's board of directors. In order to avoid conflicts of interest, the representatives of the private banks do not have the right to elect the president of each regional bank. In the eurozone, the governors of each national central bank are responsible to their national parliaments, but *only* on matters of their domestic functions—not on matters of ECB decision-making.

In a space that isn't short on paradoxes, this may be the most paradoxical aspect of the central bank's independence: their legal frameworks have created political entities—board members— whose interests and precise representative roles are impossible to characterize, let alone question. Are their interests related to monetary policy national or regional? Private or public? It makes the role (and the legitimacy) of congressional or parliamentary oversight all the more difficult to assess.

In matters of monetary policy, the parallels between the United States and Europe end at operations, or the actual making of loans and purchasing of assets. In the eurozone, the operations remain decentralized: the national central banks make the vast majority of loans and asset purchases. In the United States, ever since the Federal Open Market Committee was created in 1933, the Federal Reserve Bank of New York has executed the market transactions on behalf of the entire system. Only a few rare operations such as discounting, or more recently loans to enterprises, have been executed by regional banks. According to the European treaties, monetary policy in the eurozone is governed by the European System of Central Banks—all the central banks of each country in the European Union, regardless of whether they have adopted the euro, plus the ECB. In practice, and based on a subtle legal nuance, monetary policy operations in the eurozone are approved and implemented by the Eurosystem—that is, by the ECB and the national central banks of the eurozone. General decisions regarding monetary policy continue to be made by the ECB's board of governors, but their implementation is entrusted to these national central banks, each of which thus deals with the banks of its own country, including adapting and nationalizing the conditions for loans established by the Eurosystem's common framework.

The huge volume of loans in the Eurosystem encompasses demand from commercial banks of each country in the eurozone. That inevitably means that national central banks can, in practice, grant different volumes of loans to the private banks in their respective countries. The Eurosystem aims to make access to credit (that is, the interest rates and the conditions for the loan) as uniform as possible within the eurozone. Although it was not very explicit during the first years of its existence, the Eurosystem's role in making these conditions for credit consistent was recognized by the ECB, notably in several speeches given by the French economist Benoît Cœuré while he was a member of the ECB executive board.[16] But the difference in the volume of loans between national central banks produces imbalances, which are visible within the intra-European payment system known as Target II. A national central bank that has loaned more than the others is found to be in debt within this system.[17] In concrete terms, this results from the following mechanism: If at a certain point Belgian commercial banks need liquidity, Belgium's central bank will lend them more than usual. Therefore, the Belgian central bank increases its assets by lending to the banks and thus creates, as a counterpart, deposits for those private banks in its central bank (see earlier table 1 for a reminder of what counts for what on a central bank balance sheet). What is more, if Belgian banks are indebted to Spanish banks, they will transfer money to the latter through deposits in the central bank. Ultimately, the Belgian central bank holds the assets, and the Spanish central bank holds the deposits; it is the equivalent of a loan made by the latter to the former. Contrary to what some economists or politicians have suggested in public debate, the "imbalances within Target II," that is, the loans between central banks within the Eurosystem, do not risk dispossessing citizens of one European country while enriching another's. These loans reflect the normal functioning of a decentralized but shared monetary policy and its insurance role in a system of national central banks.[18]

THE EXTERNAL VALUE OF CURRENCY

Focusing on the central banks of the United States and the eurozone, it would be easy to forget that in history, as today, the majority of central banks manage international assets above all. Although historically these assets consisted mainly of gold, they now consist of foreign currency. The dollar and the euro are now the principal currencies held by other central banks.[19] And for their part, the Federal Reserve and the ECB, as respective issuers of dollars and euros, do not need to hold a significant amount of foreign currency because their currency is safe, accepted throughout the world, and their capital account is open.

There are two reasons why every central bank holds foreign currencies. The first is to maintain a fixed exchange rate—to keep the value of the national currency stable in relation to another currency (or a set of other currencies). The goal of fixed exchange rates relative to foreign currencies is a political matter decided upon by governments. But the central bank—or, in some countries, like the United States and the United Kingdom, another specialized institution that serves as an exchange-stabilization fund—is the institution that sells or buys the foreign currency in order to maintain the stable rate. In extreme cases, it may be that holding a stock of foreign currency is absolutely necessary to guarantee confidence in a national currency: Economic agents may only accept the currency if they know they can exchange it for dollars or euros at the central bank.[20] These extreme cases are rare, but today many countries prefer to have a fixed or relatively stable exchange rate, even if they do not officially announce it.[21]

For a central bank, the second justification for holding foreign currency is related to the possible presence of capital controls—the anticipation that foreign-capital flows might dry up and that governments and national businesses might have difficulties obtaining foreign currencies on the international markets. In these cases, the central bank's insurance function is to provide these foreign currencies to economic agents within their national borders when they are needed. That might be to importers who need to pay in foreign currency for the goods that they consume, or to companies that are in debt in a foreign currency and have to repay the loan in the same currency. In an ideal world of liberalized financial markets, it would always be possible for companies to borrow foreign currency abroad. But in reality, many countries still have capital controls in place that limit financial flows, and international financial movements are very volatile; the conditions for a small country to obtain a loan can change rapidly.

As with foreign assets purchased under the guise of monetary policy, a central bank's holding of foreign currencies can raise political questions that it has to answer. In principle, the quantity of foreign currency held by the central bank depends in part on the desired value of the exchange rate. When, in the course of history, the central banks had to hold gold in proportion to the bills that they issued, the proportional relationship between the gold and the bills was determined by the government and codified in law. But the choice of an exchange rate does not automatically determine the amount of foreign reserves, still less their allocation. Is the accumulation of exchange reserves maintained at the

expense of the financing of the national economy? Which particular currencies should be purchased? What type of financial security (stocks, private debt, or public debt)? The problem becomes
more complex when the government officially declares that the
exchange rate is free to fluctuate, but the central bank deems
(possibly an implicit agreement with the government) that it must
remain stable for the sake of monetary policy or financial stability.

Switzerland is an illustrative case of foreign-currency dynamics
in a political context. In the early 2010s, when the United States
implemented an expansionist monetary policy, Switzerland was
one of the primary countries to which private capital flowed,
largely because of the decrease in interest rates elsewhere. The
inflow of this capital increased the value of the Swiss franc relative to other currencies. To avoid an excessive appreciation of the
exchange rate, which would have greatly penalized the country's
exports, the Swiss National Bank (SNB) decided to buy foreign
financial securities (that is, to accumulate exchange reserves) in
order to decrease the value of the Swiss franc, offsetting the con-
tinuing inflow of foreign capital. In a sense, this was the equivalent
of quantitative easing policies in other countries but specific to
the context of the Swiss economy. Instead of buying government
debt to lower domestic interest rates and encourage investment
and consumption, the SNB decided to buy foreign debt to depreciate the exchange rate and stimulate Swiss exports. By 2022, the
SNB's balance sheet had grown to exceed 140 percent of the Swiss
GDP and was composed of 85 percent foreign assets rather than
domestic public debt. Without that, the Swiss economy might have
experienced an economic recession caused by a hollowing of its
national exports. The purchases of foreign currency do not officially signal the transition to a fixed exchange rate, and the Swiss
government thus had no need to make a decision in this regard.
These were simply interventions by the central bank justified by

the objectives of financial stability and economic development. This large-scale policy aroused debates in the parliament, but it was supported by the leading Swiss political parties.[22] Even so, this support did not put an end to political debate. For the central bank, the question of possible loss persists, especially since the risk is much greater with foreign assets (see chapter 3). The central bank thus had to assure the parliament that any losses would be supported by the central bank's own funds, not by Swiss taxpayers.

The fact that Switzerland is a federal country, with binding local fiscal rules, and with industries that rely heavily on exports increased the probability of political support for purchases of foreign currencies to avoid an increase in exchange rate. But that still did not preclude a debate about an alternative intervention: lowering the exchange rate through monetary creation to finance the Swiss government's debt. Doing so would have allowed the Swiss National Bank to avoid one of the primary hazards of its large investment in foreign assets, which was the use of Swiss money to finance environmentally deleterious investments internationally.[23] From the perspective of the SNB, it was partly a question of scale: Can a central bank practice its exchange policy by solely purchasing assets with a small carbon footprint? Here again we see how the situational responses of a central bank are anchored in the peculiarities of its national economic and political landscape, including the way its insurance role (which in this case involved overseeing the exchange rate) raises truly political questions about a society's organization and objectives. The case of Switzerland also illustrates the ideological vacillations of central banks and governments with regard to foreign exchange interventions and their role in a national economy. And most importantly, it speaks to the disappearance of the single model of central bank policy that was largely the convention in the 1990s.

BANKING SUPERVISION AND
MACROPRUDENTIAL POLICY

The wisdom of entrusting central banks with the role of supervising private banks has been a subject of regular debate over time.[24] Perspectives on this question have evolved considerably, and the institutions that supervise banking today are largely reflections of the history of the relationship within individual countries. Accordingly, it is difficult to articulate a single model of supervision.[25] One important reversal, however, can be observed over the course of the last three decades, one that is embodied in particular by the British and European cases and that has strengthened the role of central banks as supervisors.

It is important to note here that banking supervision is different from banking regulation. *Regulation* works through legislative changes or changes in administrative law, and it varies considerably by country. *Supervision* is the examination of banks' practices and audits of banks' accounts. Despite what the word may connote, supervision is not limited to observation, and it implies making decisions and normative choices. A supervisor may impose fines on banks, instruct them to change their practices, or organize "stress tests" based on scenarios of potential banking crises. The main goal of supervision is financial stability, that is, to avoid taking excessive risks that would lead to crises. But that is not the only goal. Supervision also implies protecting consumers and the prevention and detection of fraud. It can also ensure the effectiveness of monetary policy in fighting inflation, especially when monetary policy operations are based—as it still is in certain countries outside Europe and the United States—on changes in the value of the instruments of banking regulation, such as reserve ratios, limits on the growth of lending, or regulated deposit and lending interest rates.

Part of the role of banking supervision today is to ensure that banking regulation is respected. In most countries, banking regulation began in the 1930s and 1940s. (The United States is a notable exception, having adopted early forms of regulation during the nineteenth century, when the country did not yet have a central bank.) Before that, the central banks played an informal role as supervisors, verifying the soundness of the banks to which they lent. Similarly, central banks could organize the bailing out or restructuring of a private bank that had failed by linking it to other private banks, which would have been motivated by an interest in avoiding the contagion of a banking crisis. This informal function of supervision turned out to be broadly insufficient during the banking crises of the 1930s, and banking regulation became the norm. In a context of increased state intervention in the financial system—especially after World War II—the role of banking regulation was not limited to preserving financial stability. States could use banking regulation to guide lending and saving in the economy.[26] Thus, regulation also had a macroeconomic and a credit-policy function that it still retains today in so-called emerging countries. It was only with the movement toward financial liberalization in the 1980s and 1990s (accompanied by the Basel rules) that banking regulation became more microeconomic and centered principally on the objective of financial stability.

Whatever the goal of regulation may be, it is essential to supervise the banks' activities to be sure they are respecting the rules. This work is all the more important in a liberalized system, where financial stability requires monitoring the ways banks measure the riskiness of their financial assets. This can be extremely complex.

So should banking supervision be entrusted to the central bank or to another institution? The argument for a different supervisory system emphasizes the risk of a conflict of interest that may exist between the two types of institutions, a conflict that is potentially reinforced by personal or ideological proximities between the central bankers and private banks. The central bank might in fact be tempted to adjust its monetary policy (its interest rates, for example) in proportion to the banks' risks and profits. Another argument is based on the idea that the central bank has an interest in delaying failures or the restructuring of banks that are in poor condition so as to avoid a reputational loss for the central bank.

Alternatively, the arguments favorable to the role of the central bank in supervision stress the fact that it is indispensable that the central bank have enough information about the banks to know to which of them loans should be made in the event of a crisis. There have always been differences of opinion between countries regarding these choices. In 1996, economists Charles Goodhart and Dirk Schoenmaker wrote that a British tradition, favorable to supervision by the central bank, was opposed to a tradition present in Germany and Scandinavia, which favored separation. Many countries had a hybrid system, including Japan, where an independent authority is in charge of decisions concerning regulation and supervision, but with an oversight role for the banks (audits of accounts and on-site visits) carried out by the central bank. However, a view unfavorable to the pooling of supervision under central banks seems to have won out intellectually during the 1990s, including in the United Kingdom, with the creation of the Financial Services Authority (FSA) in 2001. Until 2013, the FSA combined the functions of regulation and supervision. The European Central Bank was thus created without an explicit mission of supervision.

Against this background, the crisis of 2008 led to a change of doctrine in these countries, and today the central banks *are* in charge of supervision. In the United States, the role of the central bank in supervision has also been strengthened by the Dodd-Frank Act of 2010, and notably by the appointment of a vice president of the Fed in charge of this function. This change in doctrine grew from a recognition of the difficulty the central bank had in playing its role of lender of last resort during the crisis without precise and immediately available information about the banks. It was also a matter of clarifying its role as lender of last resort, notably in the case of restructuring banks that were failing (in jargon, this process is called "resolution"). Reforms concerning resolution have also been implemented to supervise the respective tasks of the government, the central bank, and private creditors in the event of the failure and bailout of the banks.[27]

Historical factors often make it so that banking supervision remains shared by multiple agencies. The central bank is frequently one of several. In the United States, the banks may also be supervised by the Comptroller of the Currency or the Federal Deposit Insurance Corporation, depending on their legal form (although the Federal Reserve today receives all the information from other supervisors). In Europe, the smallest banks (and public development banks) are still supervised by authorities within their countries, not by the ECB. This arrangement, the result of a political compromise and historical factors reflecting the high degree of specificity among certain national institutions, makes it necessary for strong cooperation between the ECB and the supervisory authorities in each country. The coordination between national and supranational institutions is further complicated by their parliamentary oversight. In the European context, this is also reflected in a re-nationalization of the parliamentary (and even governmental) oversight of the ECB, which is unprecedented and has no equivalent for monetary policy. In short, it means that the ECB can be questioned by the national parliaments. As a supervisor, the ECB is also responsible to the Eurogroup—not just the parliaments—that is, to all the finance ministers of the eurozone.

Another challenge to the efficacy and democratic oversight of banking supervision is the fact that different supervisory functions can be grouped together or separated depending on country. For example, consumer protection may be handled by the central bank alone, by another, independent institution, or both.[28] In the United States, the Dodd-Frank Act of 2010 created a Consumer Financial Protection Bureau that was independent of the Treasury and the Fed. The belief was that the function of consumer protection was too important—and too long neglected—to be entrusted to the central bank alone.[29] The US case illustrates how insufficient parliamentary oversight, as with the Congress and the Fed, can lead to the supervisor neglecting a function that is nonetheless crucial.

These examples show how the integration of banking supervision within the central banks produced a single model for how states and societies monitor private banks. Great disparities remain among countries. All the same, the use of banking regulation for macroeconomic purposes has unquestionably reappeared in countries, including those with a liberalized system in Europe and the United States. This was undertaken in the name of financial stability and under the banner of "macroprudential policy." It arose in earnest after 2008, when countries of Europe and North America were hit hard by the financial crisis, and it was therefore presented as being distinct from monetary policy. Macroprudential policy seeks to limit an excessively rapid increase of credit by using diverse regulatory tools that can be adjusted to the financial cycle. So if the macroprudential regulator decides that the risks the banks are taking by increasing their loans are too great, the regulator can force them to hold more capital in relation to their loans (a "countercyclical capital buffer"). If the banks are going too far into short-term debt to finance their loans, the regulator can force them to borrow at longer term (a "net stable funding ratio"). Or if households overall are going into too much debt in the purchase of real estate, the regulator can make these loans more restrictive, notably by limiting the loans in proportion to the value of the good purchased ("loan-to-value ratio").

Since 2021, many countries have therefore created macroprudential councils to develop a new approach to financial stability.[30] It was clear that to function, these councils had to group together all the institutions of financial regulation and supervision (financial markets, insurance, etc.) and not limit their scope to the central bank. In doing so, they certainly bettered their chances of legitimacy and efficacy. Most central banks do not have the power to modify the target ratios of banking regulation or the indebtedness of households; governments are systematically much more involved in these core metrics of macroprudential policy. Still, the composition and functioning of these councils are heavily dependent on the institutions in each country. In Europe, each country has instituted its own council, coordinated at the European level by the European Systemic Risk Board. The crisis of 2008 clearly showed that financial risks could arise for different reasons in different countries; a single policy on the promotion of financial stability would not work. The Spanish crisis was sparked by a real estate market bubble, whereas the German banks were weakened particularly by too many short-term loans on the international markets. Japan, for its part, has maintained a broad view of regulation since 2000, based largely on the grave financial crises it had experienced during the 1990s.

The power of these councils varies as much as their structure. In the United Kingdom, for example, the Financial Policy Committee can act on all the financial institutions and use regulatory ratios to limit credit and risk-taking, even targeting entire economic sectors. In the United States, the Financial Stability Oversight Council (FSOC) has the ability to conduct investigations of banks or other financial institutions and to issue recommendations—but no direct decision-making power. The weakness of the FSOC's powers in the United States shows the structural lack of coordination among its regulators, which is also reflected in the country's blockage of housing finance regulation as well as its abandoned attempt to regulate nonbanking financial institutions, such as money market funds, that have become major actors in the American financial system.[31]

But the case of the United States also reflects the extent to which the institutionalization of macroprudential policies has been largely a coordination of policies that already exist in each country. It has often proceeded from a symbolic stage-setting to show an awareness of the financial risk after the crisis of 2008, but without any broad reform of the financial system itself.[32] This is not surprising, because these institutions do not have the power to issue new laws. In these councils, systemic intervention is limited to monitoring the risks taken by existing institutions within a given regulatory context; it does not seek to determine what a resilient financial system ought to be. Today, the macroprudential approach is also applied to climate risk, especially the question of how depreciation of certain carbon assets might expose financial institutions to risk.[33] But this is not the place to reflect on the way in which the financial system should finance the ecological transition. That is a question of credit policy, as we shall see.

Some macroprudential steps have already been undertaken, but it is difficult so far to judge their efficacy since macroprudential controls were relaxed during the COVID-19 pandemic to allow broad access to credit. A central question, which is still imperfectly answered, concerns the interactions between macroprudential policy and monetary policy. By acting on the volume of credit in the economy in the name of financial stability, macroprudential buffers also have an effect on the functioning of the money markets, on the demand from households, and on the activity of enterprises. Moreover, it is notable that many macroprudential tools have had equivalents in the course of history, including their use by central banks as instruments of monetary policy to limit inflation.[34] This is still the case in many countries that have not fully liberalized their financial systems. The effect of these instruments on the credit cycle and the macroeconomic cycle is less powerful in more liberalized financial systems, where nonbanking financial actors play an important role.

When international institutions such as the International Monetary Fund began to draw up an inventory of macroprudential measures on the international level, they accordingly drew on instruments that existed long before the creation of macroprudential policy in 2010. This is the case for reserve requirement ratios (i.e., the deposits that banks were required to hold at the central bank in proportion to their assets) or the limits imposed on the growth of credit. They are generally used by central banks that still control banking regulatory instruments and use them as instruments of monetary policy or as capital control. The macroprudential turning point has thus allowed central banks to give a new legitimacy—especially in emerging countries—to measures that were earlier regarded by the IMF as too interventionist and as violating the principle of the open market. This turning point coincided with a change in doctrine concerning oversight of international financial flows in the name of macroprudential policy (discussed in chapter 3). Thus, China now justifies its control over international capital flows in the name of macroprudential policy. And it still uses reserve requirement ratios in Chinese currency and foreign currency in order to fight inflation and control capital flows, respectively. These ratios require banks to deposit part of their assets in the central bank. A decrease in the value of this ratio leads to an increase of credit in the economy and may contribute to an expansionary monetary policy stance. The case of China is symptomatic of the fact that the recent requalification of instruments of monetary policy as *macroprudential instruments* may lead to confusion regarding the actions of the central bank—and that they may prevent people from clearly understanding the interactions between monetary policy and financial stability.

CENTRAL BANKS AND THE UNAVOIDABLE NATURE OF CREDIT POLICY

In the context of central banks, the term "credit policy" often has a negative connotation. This was not always the case: for decades, the central banks used the terms "credit policy" and "monetary policy" together or even interchangeably. The Werner plan of 1971, which for the first time proposed the monetary integration of Europe, used both terms. Twenty years later, the term "credit policy" had disappeared from the European plans that led to the creation of the ECB.[35]

Milton Friedman was one of the first to define credit policy as something that existed in opposition to monetary policy—in other words, that central banks should limit themselves to the latter and never touch the former.[36] In Friedman's view, credit policy is essentially any central bank policy that affects the allocation of credit in the economy (as opposed to acting on the money supply, which was Friedman's preferred intervention). Today, economists have moved on from Friedman's belief that monetary policy is best conducted by controlling the monetary base, and there is now a consensus around the use of interest rates as the central bank's preferred instrument. Also according to this view, the central bank's operations of buying and selling financial securities so that the market interest rate is equal to the interest rate that the central bank has targeted are simultaneously supposed to be agnostic concerning the allocation of credit in the economy: The central bank acts on the amount of its balance sheet, not on its composition.

Friedman's successors thus believe that a central bank is engaging in credit policy when it deviates from this rule and chooses, on the contrary, to buy certain assets over others or to lend strategically in order to promote a given activity or institution—basically, anything outside narrow goal of influencing the market rate through open-market operations.

The desire to fully separate credit policy and monetary policy may be motivated by good intentions, and it remains useful in reminding us that a central bank is not an investment bank that could, unilaterally and without democratic legitimacy, choose who or what receives loans. But this view is also illusory, for several reasons. First of all, monetary policy has uneven distributive effects—that is, it does not have the same effects on populations and businesses as a whole. This is true even for a monetary policy that operates by changing interest rates.[37] The whole of these redistributive effects is difficult to measure exactly; they depend in particular on inequalities of wealth and inequalities of access to credit. But it is essential to recognize the existence and likelihood of the distributive effects of massive purchases of financial securities or, on the contrary, a rapid, large rise in interest rates. These effects increase with larger interventions in monetary policy, including large rate changes. Thus, the fact that a central bank does not play with the composition of its balance sheet (in order to favor certain types of loans) does not mean that its monetary policy does not favor certain enterprises or citizens. It very much does.

Second, the choice of the central bank's instruments is never completely neutral, and neither is the type of financial securities that it buys. We have already seen this non-neutrality in matters of the composition of foreign exchange reserves (chapter 4) and the question of the remuneration of the banks' deposits in the central bank (chapter 3). Today, different central banks also have different doctrines regarding the appropriateness of purchasing corporate debt and equity. When the ECB bought corporate debt, it made a commitment to do so in a way that was as neutral as possible, without favoring one company or another with respect to the market. But not all firms issue debt that can be bought by the central banks, and studies suggest that the purchase of the debt of certain corporations has allowed them to increase their dividends.[38]

In normal times, the Fed is barred from purchasing corporate debt. During the pandemic, it made these purchases only in the form of resolute support for certain enterprises (the Primary Market Corporate Credit Facility, which provided credit to employers during the first month of the pandemic), in accord and partnership with the Treasury. Purchases of corporate debt are generally used by central banks that maintain control over banking regulatory instruments, and the banks typically use them as instruments of monetary policy or as capital control. Purchases of shares are usually reserved for exchange reserves, but not always: Japan used this technique to support its economy between 2011 and 2018.[39]

The view of what constitutes a neutral instrument of monetary policy—as opposed to credit policy—has varied greatly over time. Friedman thought that a central bank that used its interest rate as a tool was engaging in credit policy (because it was acting directly on the conditions of credit in the economy, with clear distributive effects), and that only the manipulation of the monetary base was neutral. Thus, many central banks that followed Friedman's precepts during the 1960s and 1970s also used reserve requirement ratios to limit commercial banks' monetary creation by forcing them to deposit part of their liquidity in the central bank. Today, most economists see this type of instrument as a tax on banks, or as a macroprudential instrument, rather than as a legitimate monetary policy tool. In contrast, open-market operations (the purchase and sale of monetary securities), which are now considered the most neutral instrument for monetary policy intervention, were formerly seen as an undue intervention in the functioning of money markets and thus contrary to economic liberalism. Up until the 1930s and 1940s, a large proportion of central banks saw neutrality as inherent in the fact that loans were made to commercial banks only when they asked for them (*standing facility*). Today, it is clear that the choice to buy treasury bonds on the open market (and all the more when it was on a large scale, with quantitative easing) reflects a clear choice regarding what a functional financial system must be: a system based on the *repo market*, that is, on banks and nonbanking institutions borrowing from one another through short-term loans backed by treasury bills as collateral. The debates about "tiering" (chapter 3) and "helicopter money" (chapter 5) have the merit of reminding us that the central bank's choice of the instruments available to it has significant effects on the financial system and the distribution of wealth among types of institutions and individuals.

Third, the central banks' goals—the ones made explicit in legal texts—can themselves compel the central bank to implement a credit policy. Here, the illustrative case of the United States since 2008 has been the subject of much discussion.[40] In order to uphold its role as lender of last resort, the Federal Reserve started in 2008 to grant emergency loans to nonbanking institutions (in particular to the insurance company AIG) under the auspices of section 13(3) of the Federal Reserve Act. The law, which had been amended in 1932 to allow the Fed to lend to nonfinancial, essentially private, corporations during the Great Depression, was extended again in 1933 and 1934. But it was used very infrequently after the 1950s. Still, this power of the central bank seemed consistent with the objectives of full employment and financial stability that were still, respectively, explicit and implicit in the institution's mandate in 2008. Without denying that this power was definitely in agreement with the central bank's missions, the US Congress nonetheless deemed it necessary to oversee it more tightly, not only after the fact, but also before any such loans were made. After the criticism in Congress, the Dodd-Frank Act of 2010 amended section 13(3) to require government approval for these special loans. With the approval of the Treasury, the power defined in section 13(3) served as a basis for most of the Fed's programs to provide liquidity to municipalities and business enterprises during the COVID-19 crisis.[41] In practice, the Fed loaned to a financial fund specially created for the occasion (a *special-purpose vehicle*), which subsequently loaned to banks or business enterprises. The US Treasury not only approved the central bank's policy but also invested in the financial fund that the Fed managed. This financial support by the Treasury was neither financially nor legally required, but it was a political symbol that attested to the cooperation and mutual aid between the two institutions. In part because of the absence of a Treasury and a European finance minister, this type of cooperation with the central bank was not seen in Europe. But the central bank bought almost all the public debt of the countries of the eurozone, while the countries' finance ministers spent freely to finance partial activity and guaranteed bank loans.[42]

The central bank's credit policy thus took different forms in the eurozone and in the United States during the pandemic, mostly because of different legal frameworks. But crucially, a crisis is not required to justify the existence of a central bank credit policy. One of the crucial questions for central banks today concerns whether they may grant loans with privileged conditions to finance activities that fight climate change. This question is particularly pressing for central banks whose mandates feature overarching objectives of economic development or support for public policies; others have seen objectives concerning the climate written into their mandates by parliaments. In practice, the central banks of China and Japan have already extended loans at reduced interest rates for banks that pledge to finance activities with small carbon footprints. While this intervention is modest in scale, another possibility might be for a central bank to change the allocation of its assets portfolio so that it privileges debt issued by companies respecting environmental criteria.

But if the climate objective is new, this kind of operation is not: in the course of history, central banks have often afforded privileged conditions to certain sectors, particularly loans for housing, exports, and agricultural activity.[43] In chapter 5, we shall discuss the conditions this may entail today, a time when central banks are ostensibly independent. As was the case for the credit policy programs implemented in response to the pandemic, the questions that arise in thinking about central banks and climate change relate to both their democratic framework (Who decides and oversees? Must there be an agreement with the government?) and their appropriateness (Is it better for the central bank to grant special, targeted loans to a large number of banks or to support an appropriate fiscal policy by purchasing public debt?). These questions must necessarily be raised and discussed publicly if the central bank of a democratic country wishes to favor, as a matter of agenda and policy, activities related to the environment. And importantly, these questions are not limited to the composition of a central bank's portfolio but also apply to its instruments for intervention.

A final reason why central banks cannot ignore credit policy is that the central bank is essentially surrounded by it. The state intervenes in credit in many different ways, and these interventions have indirect consequences for the implementation of monetary policy—that is, on the core output of the central bank. In this way, credit policy may not be the prerogative of the central bank, but the central bank is still likely to participate in it or to cope with it. Unavoidably, monetary policy and credit policy augment one another, and the actions of a state's credit policy have consequences that affect the economy and the financial system to such an extent that the central bank cannot ignore them. That is the case for the banking regulation and the macroprudential policy presented above. And it is especially the case, in most countries, for the activities of public investment banks (chapter 1).

Nonetheless, as soon as credit policy is mentioned, the United States is generally presented as an exception to the rule, because this type of policy is seldom acknowledged politically, and the country does not have a large public investment bank. Nevertheless, its federal credit programs are numerous, and credit policy has a long history in the United States, notably in the domain of housing.[44] Today, the federal credit policy is based on direct loans from, and especially on the guarantees provided by, government-sponsored enterprises (GSEs): Fannie Mae and Freddie Mac. GSEs have private shareholders, and their actions are not explicitly coordinated with other state policies. Over time, and especially starting in the 1970s, their activity was fully integrated into US financial markets: they purchase mortgage loans and package them into mortgage-backed securities (MBS) that are issued to other financial institutions. They were at the heart of the subprime crisis in 2008 because they had both financed and securitized problematic real estate loans. Put under supervision in 2008, their reform is still pending. Thus, they are a problem for the central bank, both in terms of their financial stability and their involvement in the subprime crisis. Together they constitute both hulking artifacts of the lack of coherence and reliability in US credit policy over time *and* core components of the post-2008 economic recovery plan: in parallel with direct loans from the Treasury, the GSEs were found to produce massive stimulus effects on the US economy in the years following the 2008 crash.[45] More generally, and for decades, the asset purchases by the GSEs have shaped the economic world into which US monetary policy evolved. And in doing so, they provided a stark illustration of an unassailable truth: The interactions between credit policy (via GSEs) and monetary policy (via the Fed) are a non-negligible phenomenon in the economic cycle in the United States.[46]

While we lack equivalent quantitative investigations of these interactions in European economies (at least as far as I know), credit policy fits more naturally into the European political and institutional landscape because of the presence of large public investment banks in the majority of countries, as well as of the European Investment Bank. Similar to other public development banks on other continents, but contrary to the United States, they are not limited to housing finance. At the European level, the Juncker Plan of 2015 also created an investment fund (the European Fund for Strategic Investments) that mobilized more than 300 billion euros to attract private investments with the goal of financing priority investments. In the course of a decade, and in reaction to the economic crisis of 2008, the European public development banks rapidly augmented their balance sheets by between 50 and 100 percent.[47] Since the nineteenth century, there has been a financial link between the central banks and these public development banks, the former having often provided liquidity to the latter, in the event of need, and the two of them often worked together to define the goals of credit policy. If the European Central Bank decides to grant loans on privileged conditions for the ecological transition, it will be necessary to make the criteria agree with those for these public banks. The latter may, moreover, borrow from the ECB.

The interactions between the policies of the central banks and other dimensions of credit policy are thus numerous, and they are often insufficiently understood and appreciated. The central bank's task is not to take responsibility for the whole of credit policy, because neither its modes of intervention nor its legal framework is suitable for doing that. But denying the existence of the consequences of the central bank's action on credit policy, and vice versa, whether intended or not, risks incoherence between public policies. Such an incoherence exposes nations to the risks of financial instability, and it may damage the effects of monetary policy, government action in supporting investment, and access to credit. Reconstructing the coherence of credit policy (and the central bank's role in it) is not an attack on the independence of the central banks; instead, it is today a preliminary condition for conceiving their legitimacy and their limits. On this basis, the following chapter seeks to rethink democratic oversight of central banks.

Democratizing the Central Banks

Financial liberalization and the new legal independence of many central banks during the 1990s and the early 2000s gave rise to all manner of delusions among economists in wealthy countries. The belief in the self-regulation of markets and limited central bank interventions produced a new philosophy: central banking was a purely technical task that could and should be separated from democratic discussion. The influential German economist Rudiger Dornbusch celebrated this emerging consensus during the creation of the European Central Bank: "The ECB is a monument to the proposition that money is too serious to be left to politicians: in these matters there is no such thing as a responsible politician; democratic money is bad money."[1]

THE DEAD END OF ECONOMIC CONSTITUTIONALISM

Dornbusch was deeply scarred by the economic instability he had seen in parts of South and Central America during the 1990s and he believed in the promises that financial liberalization could offer against corruption and nepotism. Dornbusch was mistaken, however, in blaming democracy for errors that were actually attributable to very undemocratic practices.

In fact, central bank independence can be justified on the grounds of democracy. It only requires that we adapt our traditional framework to finally end the illusion of the self-regulation of markets and the purported neutrality of central banks in markets' functioning. In other words, let's consider the independence of central banks without presupposing that their independence also sought to separate monetary policy from democracy.

At the same time that Dornbusch was writing, another important economist, Joseph Stiglitz, was providing a different but at the time minority perspective based on his experience as an adviser to the president of the United States in the 1990s. Stiglitz began with propositions that now seem obvious given the development of the policies of the central banks so far in the twenty-first century: "The ostensible reason for delegating responsibility to a group of experts is that the decisions are viewed to involve largely technical matters in which politics should not intrude. But the decisions made by the central bank are not just technical decisions; they involve trade-offs, judgments about whether the risks of inflation are worth the benefits of lower unemployment. These trade-offs involve values."[2] Dornbusch's and Stiglitz's opposing positions, clearly formulated before the 2008 crisis but both endorsing the principle of an independent central bank, still structure the debate today.[3] Paradoxically, each takes as its starting point Stiglitz's observation regarding the value judgments on which the central bank's decisions are based.

Some experts maintain that everything must be done to limit the intrusion of values in monetary policy decisions. In this view, the delegation of the power given to the central bank must be extremely restrictive, precisely defining the bank's objectives and the hierarchy of choices it is allowed to make. Others view this as an impossible and unacceptable constraint. The central bank's legitimacy cannot be based solely on the narrow delegation of power made to it; it must also be based on the process of deliberation and explication of the values that lead to making choices within the mandated framework.

Both positions recognize the need to assign mandates to independent central banks and the necessary transparency of the decision-making process that the central bank's respect for this mandate implies. But Dornbusch sees *delegation* as the most important criterion, whereas Stiglitz emphasizes *deliberation*. In the ideal of pure delegation that characterizes the first approach, what is essential is the definition of the central bank's mandate, which is anchored in the law. The transparency of the implementation of monetary policy and the central bank's communication are only means for signaling that the mandate is being respected to the letter. This transparency is itself technical in nature (how best to explicate the central bank's action), and thus principally unidirectional (from the central bank toward the financial markets and citizens). Parliamentary supervision of the central bank is also conceived as surveillance to ensure that the mandate is respected but not as a site of discussion or political coordination.

Stiglitz's ideal of deliberation, on the contrary, recognizes the importance of the legal framework but considers it insufficient from the outset. Legitimacy is formulated in institutions' ability to organize deliberation so that the decisions made are justified not as the application of an obvious technical fact but as the result of a choice among several possible positions whose social and economic consequences have been made explicit.

The significant disparity between these two positions brings us back to the question of values that Stiglitz posed. In Dornbusch's ideal of pure delegation, the independent authority must never make a decision that would implicate values not mentioned in its mandate. Paul Tucker, one of the most ardent defenders of this position in the domain of the central banks today, has established principles for this manner of delegation. One of Tucker's principles holds that the directors of the central bank, because they are not elected, must not make "big choices on society's values or that materially shift the distribution of political power."[4]

But how is it possible to establish a mandate that anticipates all the complex situations and value conflicts that might confront an independent authority like a central bank? In practice, this thorny question has only two possible answers: Either it is a matter of establishing a rule that is so precise that the central bank operates almost on autopilot (as John B. Taylor recommends);[5] or the law produces an extremely abstract statement that makes it possible to not hamper the principles of economic liberalism before the fact.

Generally, the second option is chosen. Except for the reference to price stability, the central banks' mandates are, as we have seen, extremely broad and subject to interpretation. While that might seem to invalidate the pure theory of delegation championed by Dornbusch, the abstractness of the rule has in fact, and somewhat paradoxically, become a key element of a view of democracy marked by "economic constitutionalism." To put it in simpler terms: those who defend a pure view of delegation and a technical view of economic policy ultimately come to claim very abstract legal principles and mandates of delegation.

In its extreme version, the theory of delegation comes down to Dornbusch's proposal quoted above and to the "economic constitutionalism" that was influential among economists and some jurists in the 1980s and 1990s.[6] Pushed to the extreme, this view leads to an abandonment of the democratic idea. Economic constitutionalism is inspired by Friedrich Hayek's notion that democracy must be protected from itself by what he calls a "demarchy," in which the "power [of the majority] would be limited by the principle that it possessed coercive power only to the extent that it was prepared to commit itself to general rules."[7]

But as political theorist Pierre Rosanvallon shows, these general rules are ultimately only abstract principles that give precedence to the functioning of the economic market over any social demand.[8] According to Rosanvallon, this abstraction and the priority it gives to the market ultimately make democracy illusory by denying the exchange of points of view and the expression of the diversity of values that are central to democracy.

Historical analysis shows how unrealistic the ideal of economic constitutionalism is, in part because the practices of the central banks have so often been disconnected from their legal framework. The evolution of monetary policy since 2008 has once again reminded us that even if it serves as a guide, the central bank's mandate as defined in legal authorities cannot anticipate all decisions needed to maintain macroeconomic and financial stability. There is no such thing as a narrow mandate or a complete contract for central banks.

The central bank's mandate—that is, the legal contract that connects it with democratic political power—is thus fundamentally incomplete because it does not specify all the central bank's rules of action in regard to possible economic situations. Even if there is agreement regarding general objectives and the set of tools available to realize them (interest rates, open-market operations, etc.), it is impossible to predict all the contingencies and to conceive a rule of monetary policy that would automatically apply in all situations. A rule that determines the central bank's interest rate according to its macroeconomic objectives can serve as a useful guide for its decision-making, but it says nothing about the type of operations that the central bank should put in place, how to stabilize financial markets, or how to avoid a public debt crisis. Central banks need rules of conduct so that their social objectives are clear and no suspicion of conflict of interest arises. But the way these rules are applied in practice leaves room for many possible options that should be subject to deliberation—informed by expertise—and checks and balances. In addition, as Stiglitz's remarks remind us, an automatic monetary policy rule presupposes constant values and a consensus regarding macroeconomic objectives. This is plainly not the case: economists debate endlessly whether it is better to target the inflation rate or the nominal GDP, what the appropriate definition of the unemployment rate is, or what definition of consumer prices should be the central bank's objective (including or excluding energy, for example). This list goes on. It would be illusory to claim that there is complete agreement about the questions, let alone their answers.

In the course of the preceding chapters, we have seen that the central banks have been forced to constantly adapt to unforeseen events and to invent new strategies and tools in order to achieve their objectives. Nothing was written in advance. Economists who have studied incomplete contracts point out that the fundamental question is who has the right to make decisions about the "missing things" in the contract.[9] The answer to this question cannot, obviously, be the same as it would be in a business enterprise, where ownership of capital is usually accompanied by the right to decide. Ours is not a business but a democratic society. And conferring on central bankers the ability to decide alone what are the "missing things" exceeds the mandate that was entrusted to them by the people's representatives.

The difficulty of defining the central banks' democratic legitimacy is twice as great when they are charged with supervising private banks. Monitoring banks, like monitoring monetary policy, poses democratic challenges in terms of independence. Thus, the reintegration of banking supervision into the role of central banks after the 2008 crisis also raised institutional questions. The European Central Bank, for example, explicitly implemented a "principle of separation" to ensure that the process of making decisions about monetary policy would be separated from supervision, with different time frames and staffs.[10] The independence of banking supervision requires even stricter parliamentary oversight. It is in fact very difficult, in matters of supervision, to identify precisely the objective that is to be achieved and that is observable by the parliament. The goal is to avoid a financial crisis. But the supervisor must also be able to render an account of the criteria used and their evolution over time in order to enable the parliament to assess the consistency between means and ends.[11] Obviously, there are criteria and rules that guide banking supervision. But the evolution of banking supervision in response to changes in the sector and the financial environment cannot depend on a mathematical formula written beforehand in the text of the laws.

DELIBERATION AND REFLEXIVITY

Acknowledging that the independence of central banks has historically been more a question of practice than of law (detailed in chapter 4), one has no choice but to reject the notion that a legal statute and a clear and precise mandate can suffice to ensure the central bank's legitimacy. That is why I now turn to the other philosophical tradition of democracy that gives a role to independent central banks while emphasizing the *processes of deliberation and reflexivity* that must accompany independence. This intellectual tradition, while recognizing the important role played by delegation, acknowledges from the outset that even a detailed and specific mandate will not prevent significant, value-based choices from being made that have a major impact on social and economic arrangements. The political legitimacy of delegation comes as much from the way that it is justified and debated as it does from the initial mandate, which is necessarily too vague and too narrow all at once.

Rosanvallon, who defends this conception of democracy, has devoted much of his work to reflecting on the democratic legitimacy of independent authorities such as central banks. He stresses the importance of making "reflexivity and impartiality qualities that are constantly being put to the test before the eyes of the public"; "it is from an organized confrontation between rulers, with a contradictory understanding of the world, that democracy will increasingly be nourished."[12] How do we set up institutions that will allow us to make the central banks' independence compatible with such principles?

The deliberative view of the central bank's independence articulated by Stiglitz and Rosanvallon among others has recently been taken up by jurists and political scientists.[13] Research in this area is mainly normative, making use of theoretical reflections on democracy, but it is also based on a sociological and legal critique of the weak oversight exercised by parliaments over central banks.

The legal independence of the central bank in relation to the government also affords the central bank the right to disobey the government in the name of pursuing the objectives—however general and relatively vague—that are assigned to it by law or by the constitution. This independence is not intrinsically contrary to democracy because it follows from a decision and a vote of the people's representatives. The will of the people defines it, and it is revocable. But it can only be justified by a conception that does not reduce democratic legitimacy to elections and representation. The bank's independence is based on the idea that democracy is a superior system of government because it makes it possible to arrive at better decisions through the balance of powers and the expression of diverse opinions. In other words, the justification of the independence of an administrative authority is founded on an *epistemic* conception of democracy, which recognizes that some political decisions do not necessarily depend on the immediate result of elections and that they can be justified by a substantial level of expertise.[14] If, on the contrary, we maintain that only the representatives elected at a given moment have the power to make such decisions, then only they can make decisions legitimately. In that case, independent authorities—the constitutional court, the central bank, the competition authority, the media regulatory authority, and other authorities—have no reason to exist. Thus, there can be no independence without the mechanisms that guarantee, on the one hand, that the decisions made by the independent authority are in accord with the objectives that have been assigned to it by law, and on the other hand, that these same decisions are the result of deliberations presenting diverse, opposing, impartial, and reflective points of view. In both cases, only parliamentary oversight and the consideration of divergent interests make it possible to avoid the flaws that can lead to arbitrariness or to the dictatorship of unelected experts. Asking the central bank to present its decisions transparently is not sufficient. Deliberation does not exist without contestation, and reflexivity cannot be a self-centered practice.[15] Justifying independence solely on the basis of delegating power of the people's representatives neglects the importance of deliberation in democratic legitimacy.

These arguments show the need to institutionalize deliberation (or reflexivity) on monetary policy in order to restore its democratic legitimacy. In other words, an exchange of perspectives and a critical examination of choices affecting monetary policy need to take place within an institution outside the central bank. The next section seeks to imagine such an institutional system in the case of Europe before turning to the United States.

THE EURO'S DEMOCRATIC DEFICIT

The problem that the ECB faces when it comes to democracy is that it is both judge and party to the interpretation of its mandate. The discussion of the central bank's choices, whether past or future, takes place almost exclusively internally. When the bank communicates to the political representation—the parliament—it does so as a fait accompli.

The mandate of the European System of Central Banks (ESCB) is to "support the general economic policies in the EU with a view to contributing to the achievement of the Union's objectives as laid down in Article 3 of the Treaty on European Union" and to do so "without prejudice to the objective of price stability." This article 3 stipulates that the European Union "shall work for the sustainable development of Europe based on balanced economic growth and price stability, a highly competitive social market economy, aiming at full employment and social progress, and a high level of protection and improvement of the quality of the environment." The law therefore opens the door to all manner of actions on the part of the central bank, including even a potentially unlimited "decommodification" to support social and environmental policies. But as we saw earlier, decommodification is a matter of degree—how vulnerable people are to the whims of markets. Today's general framework remains, resolutely, one of a market economy with a private financial system. The European treaty reaffirms this in a tempered form: "The ESCB shall act in accordance with the principle of an open market economy with free competition, favoring an efficient allocation of resources" (Treaty on the Functioning of the European Union, article 127).

If the central bank clings to a laissez-faire approach to the market, it fails to uphold the role entrusted to it through its mandate, and thereby put social progress, the environment, or monetary and financial stability at risk. And if it tries to substitute itself for the market in the role as lender, it breaks with the principle of the market economy promoted by the European Union, effectively dissolving its raison d'être as a central bank and transforming itself into a public investment bank.

The mandate is thus extraordinarily vague and general: each of its terms leaves considerable room for interpretation and maneuvering. In 2003, the ECB explained to the public that the objective of price stability had to be interpreted as an average inflation greater than, but close to, 2 percent of the annual growth of the harmonized index of consumer prices. In June 2021, this objective was revised and is now "2% over the medium term," thus tolerating temporary spikes beyond the inflation target. During the first decade (at least) of the eurozone's existence, the ECB undoubtedly favored an interpretation of its mandate that emphasized the market economy imperatives more than the other possible dimensions of the European policy, asking governments to implement "structural reforms" that sought to liberalize, in a uniform way, the labor market or the financial markets, arguing that this would facilitate the implementation of its monetary policy.[16] This choice, along with other similar declarations from the ECB, reflected a European political consensus that gave priority to the market economy over other possible imperatives. Yet this was never explicitly situated as a consideration of democratic legitimacy.

So long as the Eurosystem's activity was discreet and oriented toward the market economy, and so long as its insurance function continued in the background, few people worried about how the ECB's actions and public pronouncements reflected on its democratic legitimacy. But all that changed starting with the crisis in 2008, when the central bank's insurance function was first fully activated. The intertwining of the central bank's decisions with the functioning of the welfare state and its objectives moved to the forefront, as did the absence of any genuinely democratic dialogue.

Thus, over the last decade the ECB has justified new actions by producing new interpretations of its mandate. This was notably the case for purchases of public debt, as detailed in chapter 3. More recently, the ECB put forward a principle called "market neutrality" to justify its purchases of public and private debt while still respecting the principle of free competition (that is to say that it buys these assets in proportion to their issuance on the markets and the composition of the ECB's capital). But more recently, it has suggested that this principle of "market neutrality" must be challenged because it encourages the purchase of financial assets in polluting companies—in the same proportion as the financial markets—and thus contradicts the central bank's "support for the European Union's general policies."

During the pandemic, the ECB further clarified the support it provides to the EU by announcing that its policy should henceforth provide states access to favorable financing conditions. The ECB's interpretation of its own mandate, articulated in such announcements, has a way of arousing expectations and enlivening discussions in the press and in financial circles. For banks and financial institutions, interpreting the slightest remarks written or uttered by the central bankers has become a full-fledged vocation ("ECB watchers"). In this ecosystem, we have thus become accustomed to the central bank's authorship of its own interpretation of its mandate. The only other major site of debate regarding the interpretation of the central bank's mandate is the Court of Justice of the European Union (CJEU), in particular when it is required to rule on a complaint filed against the ECB. The CJEU has so far validated the ECB's political choices, but it has also strongly reminded the central bank that it has "the obligation to examine, with care and impartiality, all the pertinent elements of the situation involved and to motivate its decisions in a sufficient way." All the same, before the CJEU stage, there is no institution mandated to ensure that the ECB shows impartiality and sufficiently justifies its decisions. The European Parliament has an extremely limited role in the supervision of the ECB and the discussion of monetary policy. The ECB presents its annual report to the parliament once a year, and the parliament can summon the representatives of the ECB at any time of the year (for the "monetary dialogue," which is trimestral) or address written questions to them.[17]

Observers of this monetary dialogue typically offer the same assessment: It is mainly an after-the-fact explication of the ECB's policy and a mainly formal dialogue to which the ECB can respond in a very general manner.[18] In addition, there is no connection between the European dialogue and the dialogues that may occur between national parliaments and the national central banks within the Eurosystem. Since it is often said that monetary policy is at the forefront of European integration, we might find it surprising that the partly decentralized (but harmonized) system of the Eurosystem's monetary functioning is not better connected with parliamentary dialogues. Here the important work done by the European Parliament's Committee on Economic and Monetary Affairs must be acknowledged, in particular the way the committee has pushed the ECB to be more transparent or, in the case of the troika, showed that the central bank had exceeded its boundaries.[19] The committee's work, however, is limited in scope: it does not have the ability to gather dissenting points of view on monetary policy and financial questions from society at large, or to produce scenarios of economic policy that might provide the basis for an investigation into the medium- to long-term consequences of the ECB's policies, including how its policies interact with other credit policies of the European Union.

THE FLAWS IN THE EUROPEAN DIALOGUE

Several proposals have already been formulated with the goal of improving the quality of the ECB's dialogue with the parliament and strengthening the parliament's role in it. In particular, a proposal has been floated to create a subcommittee within the European Parliament's Committee on Economic and Monetary Affairs that would be devoted entirely to dialogue with the ECB, including a requirement that the European Parliament and the European Council draw up an annual list of the main objectives that the ECB should achieve.[20]

It is important to go further. Studies on deliberation in modern democracies teach us that their quality is based on equal access to information, as well as on equal and substantial treatment of diverse points of view.[21] In this perspective, the dialogue between the Eurosystem and the European Parliament is currently of insufficient quality for at least three reasons: First, there is a disparity in the information and expertise at the disposal of the central bank and those available to the parliament (and more generally to society at large). The ECB produces subtle analyses of the economic climate, of financial stability, and of monetary policy, thanks to the more than four hundred economists that it employs full time.[22] If we also include the economists employed in the various national central banks, this figure would at least double, and it is comparable to the current number in the United States.

The parliament, by contrast, relies exclusively on short reports commissioned from outside economists (who do not work full time for the institution), generally four of them for each trimestral dialogue. This institutional imbalance reflects a growing concern among economists: the problem of the dominance of the statistics and economic analyses and research produced by the central banks themselves. While the substantial growth in the number of economists and in the quality of the research within the central banks over the last two decades has certainly increased knowledge about financial stability and monetary policy, it has also created a risk that these institutions might monopolize the debate on these subjects.

A sociological study of this trend revealed that almost half the research articles published on monetary policy are written by at least one economist at a central bank.[23] Articles written by economists at the central banks, moreover, clearly put more emphasis on the positive (and expected) effects of monetary policy than do those written by academics.[24] Given the uncertainty present in even the most rigorous economic studies—and accordingly how the narrative surrounding the study can have a substantial impact on its reception—it is not difficult to imagine that central banks, even if staffed with the best economists, might be reluctant to publish research results that run counter to their expectations.

Second, the ECB's typical responses to parliamentary inquiry—even if their form and content have varied over time and depending on the persons—are typically too general to allow us to conclude that this "dialogue" reflects a balance between the parties. Above all, the ECB is in a position to justify its own choices, not in an authentic dialogue in which the parliament would present political alternatives that the ECB could refute or include in its own thought. The absence of equal treatment afforded to the arguments of the different parties eliminates any possibility of coordination between the general policies of the Union and the policy of the ECB, even though the European treaties commit the bank to support the EU. In this sense, the ECB is both judge and party to its own policy.

Finally, the third reason for the mediocre quality of the debate is the absence of a diversity of points of view. The European Parliament's Committee on Economic and Monetary Affairs does not have the means to systematically collect the points of view expressed by various interest groups, nongovernmental organizations, or countries whose interests are within the scope of the ECB's impact. There is no connection between the testimony of central bankers at the national parliaments' hearings and the European parliamentary dialogue. The reports that experts draft for the Parliamentary Committee cannot suffice to give an equal voice to different points of view.

In a praiseworthy development, in 2020 the ECB launched an initiative called "ECB Listens," which was intended to invite a great diversity of questions about and criticisms of its policies. But, as in the case of economic expertise, this amounted to internalizing the criticism. It is the ECB itself that organizes the dialogue and the way in which it can collect, present, and analyze outside points of view. (Since 2019, the US Federal Reserve has organized a similar initiative: "Fed Listens.")

A final problem that the ECB confronts regarding the expression of points of view has to do with the lack of diversity among its directors, who are largely elderly white men. This problem has been raised and discussed, including by the ECB itself, in particular concerning the inadequate presence of women. This, notably, is also a larger problem across the field of economics.

A EUROPEAN CREDIT COUNCIL

The structural flaws in the dialogue between the parliament and the ECB call for the construction of a new institutional framework, one that makes it possible to rebalance the policy deliberation led by the ECB. Such a framework must endow the parliament (and more broadly, all the European legislative and executive powers) with an economic expertise—enabling it to begin a structured dialogue on the objectives of monetary policy, the means of achieving them, and above all, the consequences of the ECB's policy for the other policies of the European Union, including the connections between them.

This dialogue must also allow the parliament to account for input from different sectors of economic activity and countries. From this broader dialogue, a coordination between monetary policy and fiscal policy, or environmental policy, could emerge. And it would be even stronger and more fruitful if the legislative power and legitimacy of the European Parliament were reinforced in the course of its restructuring.[25]

Several institutional arrangements are possible. They might include an administrative agency that reports directly to the parliament, along the model of the Congressional Budget Office in the United States, or one that sits jointly in the European Commission and the parliament; a segment of the economists who work today at the ECB or in the national central banks could move to this institution. Even as it preserves the independence of the central bank, this institution would be inspired in part by the credit councils established in several European countries after World War II; this would facilitate the coordination of monetary policy not only with fiscal policies but with public investment policies and industrial policies as well.

A European Credit Council would also make it possible to coordinate the various interests that seek to ensure that the general objectives of the European Union are financed. To ensure that monetary policy can support "the protection and improvement of the quality of the environment," it is critical to determine how the ECB's credit policy can participate in the financing of this objective—whether it is necessary, and, consequently, how it must connect with the policies of environmental financing by other European institutions (the European Investment Bank, the European Development Fund, the European Agricultural Guarantee Fund, the European Commission, among others). This would also require the institutional ability to formulate scenarios based on quantitative models and legal and political analyses, especially those that shed light on alternative economic policies and possible interactions among monetary policy, the sustainability of public debts, and the financing of the Union's other major objectives.

The ECB would derive, and indeed ensure, the legitimacy of its decisions from the reflexivity and consultation facilitated by this council. In terms of democratic practice, a notable consequence would be removing the burden of proof around price stability and the priority bestowed on it. In other words, if the credit council formulates precise credit policy measures with a message that those measures support the EU's general objectives, then the burden would be on the ECB to respond by clarifying the possible impacts on price stability, including the criteria it used to evaluate those impacts.

The proposal to establish a European Credit Council thus has two goals: First, it seeks to strengthen the parliament's oversight of the central bank—and thus the parliament's power and the central bank's legitimacy—by making it possible to rebalance expertise and to engage in deliberation that takes into account alternative scenarios (not just the scenarios described by the ECB). The objective is to make the ECB's interpretation of its mandate justifiable through a process that demonstrates that it has examined all the possible options and reflected on its choices. In doing so, the ECB could pride itself on the legitimacy of its decisions, reached in cooperation with the parliament—and subjected to the different opinions in the society solicited by the credit council. The Court of Justice of the European Union would necessarily rely on this deliberative process in ruling on whether the decisions made by the ECB accord with its objectives and conform with the general policies of the European Union as formulated by the parliament and the Council of the European Union.

This second goal of the credit council is to create a place where the policies of the different European agencies participating in credit policy, including the central bank, are coordinated. This would include at least the European Commission, the European Investment Bank (EIB), the ECB, and the European association of long-term investors (i.e., public development banks). The credit council's task would be twofold: First, to provide expertise for the parliament and to present divergent views so that the parliament can make proposals regarding credit policy; and second, to publish reports validated by each institution that reflect the shared aims of their policies.

The credit council would thus not play a decision-making role. And the ECB would not answer to this council, but still to the parliament. Crucially, this council would not replace a parliamentary committee and would not be responsible for supervising the ECB and other institutions. The institutional value resides in the fact that it would provide the parliament with independent studies that would enable the parliament to strengthen its control over the ECB and the EIB; the council would be a place where the existing institutions are coordinated. In this role, it is also essential to separate the two primary functions of the council: the council's personnel would have to respond to the parliament's requests without interference by the representatives of the institutions (the ECB, the EIB, among others) that might have seats on its board of directors.

TAKING CRITICISM INTO ACCOUNT

Not everyone favors the greater democratization of European monetary policy. Some specialists in the history of European integration, in particular Giandomenico Majone and Andrew Mora-vcsik, have described as a "myth" the argument that the European Union functions less democratically than the national states in Europe.[26] This debate flared in the course of the first decade of the twenty-first century.

According to these two political scientists, the independence of the central bank with regard to the parliament (as well as that of the Union's other authorities, including the European Commission) reflects, on the contrary, the truly democratic nature of the European Union. For Majone, the EU is concerned solely with directives that have little concrete impact on citizens—hence the necessity of a legitimacy based on its expertise rather than on the outcomes of voting and the consideration of different points of view.

For Moravcsik, the EU is a political entity that functions in an intergovernmental manner: its structure gives the national governments the last word. The individual countries delegate to the independent institutions only the policies that they cannot implement at the national level. These intergovernmental institutions, beneficially, are more transparent and less subject to lobbying than the national parliaments and governments. Moravcsik agrees with Majone in defending the bureaucratic and technocratic character of the EU. Both strongly oppose the notion, defended chiefly by the EU's social-democratic theoreticians, including Jürgen Habermas and Fritz Scharpf, who argue that Europe should be repoliticized and democratized.[27]

From Majone and Moravcsik's point of view, it would be vain or even dangerous to attempt to increase deliberation concerning monetary policy. The institutionalization of an impartial, substantial, and informed debate regarding the action of the central bank merely offers a deliberative veneer that would have, at best, no real impact on the choice of monetary policy and might even risk weakening the ECB's decisions by exposing them to unproductive criticism or slowing them down.

Majone and Moravcsik's approach *does* have the advantage of showing that the EU's functioning is unique, that the independence of the administrative authorities is consistent with the European political project, and that the organization of the EU's institutions does in fact take on a more democratic character than that of many of the national parliaments and governments in Europe, especially when it comes to the transparency and manner in which its decisions are arrived at.[28] Nevertheless, these authors' approach has obvious limits, and Majone and Moravcsik's arguments have been criticized in two principal ways.[29] In the first place, the decisions made by independent European authorities have redistributive and political consequences that are much more consequential than these authors admit. As this book has shown, this assertion is undeniable given the evolution of monetary policy in the EU and elsewhere since 2008. As political scientist Antoine Vauchez has argued, European political integration—especially in response to the events of 2008–2010—is evolving in a way that goes far beyond the simple regulatory role that Majone and Moravcsik attribute to the EU.[30]

The events of the past decade have created a situation that these two authors (and many political decision-makers) did not foresee. The rapid development of European integration that has taken place since 2008, and especially the various mechanisms of common insurance that have been established (detailed in chapters 2 and 3—the solidarity funds, the European Stability Mechanism, the central bank's purchase of public debt, among others) have made a depoliticized view of the EU wholly untenable.

A second flaw in Majone and Moravcsik's position may be found in their argument that EU policy decisions would not be affected by better-organized deliberation and consideration of criticisms—

what Rosanvallon has called "reflexive legitimacy"—because of the outsize influence of intergovernmental negotiations. Deliberation and reflexivity are only pointless if we assume that citizens and leaders come into the debate with prejudiced and fixed preferences regarding the political choices on the table.

On the contrary, deliberation would have a significant impact on the decision-making process, for several reasons. First, by amplifying the information concerning monetary policy at the disposal of citizens and members of parliament, it would change the terms of public debate, including the agenda and the questions that the ECB must answer. (This would follow the example of the questions raised about climate change and inequalities, issues on which the central banks have been forced to take a position, though not without difficulty.)

In addition, by placing the burden of proof on the ECB, deliberation would force the central bank to develop arguments it would otherwise not have made—and certainly not articulated. It can lead to decisions that would not have been considered without a more balanced and reflexive institutional presentation of arguments. In practical terms, deliberation can be understood as a way of obeying and putting into practice the ruling of the Court of Justice of the European Union, which stressed that the European System of Central Banks is under the "obligation to examine carefully and impartially all the relevant elements of the situation in question and to give an adequate statement of the reasons for its decisions."[31]

Except when it is applied to justice itself, "impartiality" in this context is a completely relative concept (without even mentioning the "care" required). It is only when real debate takes place, with informed, divergent points of view, that the impartiality and motivation of a decision can be assessed. Contrary to what has happened more often, a debate in the parliament might also keep the discussion of the legitimacy of monetary policy from being sent back to the national constitutional courts.[32]

Furthermore, deliberation is a step toward coordination. In the case of monetary policy, coordination with other policies (related to budget, wages, the environment, etc.) means shared objective-setting and drawing up roadmaps to reach those objectives. Such a debate might also enable the European Parliament to take up the powers regarding the implementation of monetary policy that are at its disposal but which it does not use. This concerns in particular the possibility of granting the ECB the right to use other instruments of monetary policy, in addition to loans to the banks and the purchase of assets.[33]

A final objection to the principle of reflexivity concerns its risk of ineffectual procedures. On this point, we must be precise lest there be any doubt: the operational independence of the central bank is and must remain an imperative. As we have seen in chapter 1, the role of a central bank is to intervene in the markets in order to avoid a financial crisis (or an exchange rate crisis in countries with fixed exchange rates). These interventions, which are effective only when they are immediate, must be able to be conducted without uncertainty regarding their legal status. But it is also true that the long-term management of assets bought to guarantee financial stability, as well as the conditions for loans, must be subjected to democratic debate.

Some will worry about the reactions of financial markets to these debates. As these markets are accustomed to (over)reacting to every announcement or publication of statistics from the ECB, one might reasonably assume that some investors won't miss the opportunity to use the terms of the parliamentary debates to try to predict the decisions of the central bank. This imposes a need on the central bank to amend its communications in order to orient financial markets to this new form of deliberation. One can imagine worse things.

THE DEBATES IN THE UNITED STATES

The proposed European Credit Council that I have outlined in some respects resembles the US Congressional Budget Office (CBO), which is an arm of Congress that produces independent analyses of budgetary and economic issues. Its analyses are made available for use during fiscal deliberations in Congress, and they are neither recommendations nor decisions: they are independent analyses of costs, both financial and otherwise, surrounding proposed legislation. In the same spirit as the European Credit Council, it is valuable to consider expanding the functions of the CBO to create a sister institution on money and credit. Under this arrangement, the CBO could serve multiple roles: it could formulate alternative scenarios of monetary policy, which Congress could use during its hearings on the Federal Reserve; it could also conduct studies on the distributive consequences of the Fed's policies and on the interactions between monetary policy and other US credit policies (including federal loans and the activities of GSEs like Fannie Mae and Freddie Mac; see chapter 4). In this context, the CBO's studies have thus far been limited to federal loans.[34] As in the case of Europe, increasing the CBO's remit would also increase its expertise (that is, the number of economic experts that it employs), thus promoting a greater balance of opinion when the Fed's representatives testify before Congress. This expertise might usefully address the financial system as a whole, including the interactions between the financial system and monetary policy. That would allow Congress to take up, with adequate evidence, the question of whether the Fed's policy lends too much support to shadow banks (financial institutions that are not banks), even though such institutions are not highly regulated.[35] It could also lend its expertise to special commissions created by Congress to supervise the Fed's special activities, as was the case with the COVID-19 Congressional Oversight Commission (which independently examined the management of the common fund shared by the Fed and the Treasury that was created to assist businesses during the pandemic). The Office of Inspector General (OIG) for the Board of Governors of the Federal Reserve System is an independent oversight authority that reports to Congress and conducts investigations to prevent and detect fraud, waste, and abuse. The role of this valuable office, however, is not to suggest or model alternative policy scenarios or reforms to be discussed by the people's representatives.

Several recent studies of the US Federal Reserve share my concern about the insufficient democratic accountability of central banks. The point of these criticisms is to emphasize the need to strengthen democratic control over these institutions—to limit the zeal of the central banks, which seem to have become omnipotent, while at the same time acknowledging that the central banks' actions have been redefined over time and that there is no "return" to a narrow mandate in the offing. The laws concerning the central banks are necessarily too vague and too subject to interpretation to allow us to think that we can simply deduce, without balanced deliberation, a correct way to proceed.[36] Legal scholars Peter Conti-Brown and David A. Wishnick have characterized the Federal Reserve's actions, especially in contexts where its mandate is imprecise (for example, digital currency, cybersecurity, climate change), as a kind of "technocratic pragmatism." The criterion they propose to set limits to this extension of the central bank's activities is "non-coercion"—allowing the Fed to engage in these policy experiments only on subjects and with methods that do not constrain other institutions. In Conti-Brown and Wishnick's proposal, congressional oversight is critical for deciding whether the Fed is transgressing such boundaries: "technocratic pragmatism without Congressional oversight makes accountability arguments against agency experimentation damning." Even if the hearings on the Fed conducted by the US Congress are already demanding, the authors nonetheless point to their shortcomings—notably the fact that the Fed tends to take refuge behind claims of banking's inherent secrecy. Endowing Congress with a broader, stronger expertise—as I have suggested in the European case—would permit it to approach these hearings with a more holistic and systematic view of the financial system and the role of the Fed within it, as well as with a more sustained argument on the possible conflicts between the Fed's objectives and its practices.

From an opposite perspective—denouncing the Fed's activism and seeking to restrict its policy freelancing experiments—legal scholar Christina Parajon Skinner has compiled a list of questions that Congress might ask the Fed in order to assess the legitimacy of the central bank's actions.[37] She stresses in particular the necessity of discussing the way that new measures would pose the risk of conflict with other federal policies and of establishing guardrails to ensure that they will not have unforeseen consequences. But the stronger role for Congress that she calls for risks coming to naught if Congress does not have the means to produce alternative monetary policy scenarios to examine the potential unforeseen consequences.

When US experts call for greater congressional oversight of the Federal Reserve, they seldom situate their arguments in a context of what the country's credit policy ought to look like—how money and credit get allocated and to what distributional ends. But there are exceptions, including proposals that seek to establish a more ambitious (that is, formed and acknowledged) credit policy in the United States—especially for financing infrastructures and the battle against global warming—and that integrate the democratic dimension into their reflection. Legal scholar Saule Omarova, for example, has included a Public Interest Council in her proposal for a National Investment Authority (NIA).[38] Inspired by the Reconstruction Finance Corporation created by the New Deal in the United States, the NIA would resemble public investment banks in the rest of the world, including Europe (chapters 1 and 4). It would mobilize private and public funds to make long-term loans at below-market rates while accounting for the priorities determined by the legislators. Like public investment banks in Europe, the NIA would be independent from the government, in order to keep its funds from being used for partisan ends. The NIA would also have, as in Europe, access to the central bank's refinancing. Omarova's proposed Public Interest Council would allow an efficacious congressional control of this institution. Its authority would consist of monitoring and examining the NIA's practices while at the same time providing advice and deliberation (including some based on the public's request), and by articulating scenarios and recommendations regarding credit policy. The deliberative and consultative dimension of the Public Interest Council brings it closer to the European Credit Council, as does its role in providing support and ideas to Congress. However, unlike the European Credit Council, the proposal for a Public Interest Council is not intended to support congressional oversight of the Fed, nor to organize coordination of credit policy with other entities.

CLIMATE CHANGE

Having established the principles of reform for the institutional framework of monetary policy, I will now offer three examples— and suggest others—to illustrate how this new framework might lead central banks to make decisions that are at once more democratic, more aligned with their mandate, and more effective economically.

The central banks have become aware that they can no longer ignore the question of climate change. At this point, in many countries and in Europe, they recognize that they must approach this question in two ways. The first is from a perspective of financial stability. As regulators of banks and as investors, they must take into account the fact that some assets now considered safe will become riskier because of changes related to energy and the environment. They must therefore anticipate these risks, participate in the elaboration of a classification of these risks, and adapt banking regulation to them.[39] Second, the central banks have recognized that their purchases of private assets sometimes include enterprises that are highly polluting or that emit excessive CO_2, as with industry sectors like oil or chemicals. For the ECB, a formal examination of this subject is underway, acknowledging that the purchase of such assets might contravene its legal objective of supporting the EU's general policies.

However, this realization suffers from blind spots. Addressing the main issues requires coordination between the ECB and the European legislative and executive powers. A critical question is whether the ECB should incentivize financial institutions to lend more to finance ecological investment, or whether the ECB itself should contribute directly to this kind of investment. As we have seen, many taboos of central banking have been violated since 2008, including the former prohibition on making targeted loans for investment in certain sectors. In the EU, these loans (called TLTROs) have been justified by the necessity of involving all enterprises, including small- and medium-sized enterprises that continue to find it difficult to obtain loans on terms close to the ECB's lending rate.

Some might argue that so long as the energy-transition sector (projects labeled "green") does not encounter problems specific to financing, the ECB should not intervene to guarantee it access to preferential rates. The European Investment Bank, which finances the energy transition in particular, can easily be refinanced by the ECB and benefits from credit conditions on the markets as favorable as those of France or Germany. These states themselves borrow at low real interest rates and therefore should have no reason not to invest long term.

A similar objection might be levied at the ECB's potential purchase of equity in the stock market, the way the Bank of Japan has done in its real estate sector. But this argument, based solely on observations of market prices in the here and now, may reach its limits if types of long-term investment necessary for the protection of the environment are characterized by a strong uncertainty and do not fulfill the conditions for receiving financing that are based on less pressing circumstances. A similar problem arises when the ecological transition implies financial losses. This will be the case with assets that depreciate or with enterprises that are excessively polluting and that will have to close (coal-fired power plants, for example). The cost of such a transition may be very large for states or even threaten the credibility of their debt.

The central bank can play a role in the liquidation of these enterprises or polluting assets by bearing the risk in the short term and by evening out losses over the long term. It is a model similar to what was done in the United States to save AIG or in Switzerland to save the bank UBS in 2008. According to the criteria that were used to justify recent asset purchases, the central bank has grounds for intervening if there is a risk of economic crisis or financial stability. But it is clear that the central bank cannot decide on its own to engage in such an operation, nor can it choose the enterprises to be liquidated. Cooperation with the government and the parliament is not just necessary but inevitable (as it was done to save banks in 2008).

Finally, as inflation spikes again and the central bank raises interest rates, the question is whether it would be legitimate to maintain a lower interest rate on targeted loans (TLTRO) for ecological financing. Given the central bank law, the answer to this question in the EU depends on two parameters: Is investment for the ecological transition less inflationary? And how important does the EU consider its environmental objective? If the EU gives absolute priority to safeguarding the environment, and if it can be proved that environmentally sustainable investment does not contribute to rising inflation—that the privileged treatment of this sector will not lead to distortions in the competition between the enterprises that compose it—then the ECB's current mandate is not incompatible with a differentiated treatment of the refinancing of green loans by the central bank in the event of a rise in interest rates. The best argument for the green TLTRO—compatible with the ECB legal framework, official objectives, and with other EU credit policies—might be that it is necessary to insulate green investments from an increase in interest rates in order to preserve the environment and reduce future energy costs as well as our exposure to future environmental shocks that may endanger the value of money and the credit system.

But there again, this decision is well founded only if the EU clarifies its general policy objective (including, in a very technical manner, the definition of the environmental sector) and the way in which monetary policy can participate in it. It requires a coordination and a presentation of arguments and counterarguments in a democratic space—a requirement that is a few steps away from our current circumstances.

COORDINATION BETWEEN BUDGETARY POLICY
AND MONETARY POLICY

The discussion of ecological financing inevitably raises the question of the coordination between fiscal policy and monetary policy. In theory, the central bank is only a financial support for private banks, for public banks, and for states. The central bank has no competent staff for studying and choosing investments. A promise of unlimited financing of the state by the central bank not only presents a potential danger of inflation; it is also a political danger if it is thought that this financing can replace taxes or justify the abandonment of transparency and democratic criteria for choosing public investments. And if public policy has only one tool at its disposal (i.e., a fiscal policy financed entirely by issuing money), it creates an undesirable situation in which the financing of public services and public investment has to be automatically reduced or taxes increased if inflation rises, instead of a more elaborate fine-tuning that combines a change in interest rates, credit conditions, taxes, and public spending. It is for this reason that it is necessary to distinguish between monetary policy and fiscal policy. This requires an open and transparent discussion of the fiscal consequences of central bank purchases of government securities, for example, whether taxes or debt issuance are preferable in an environment of low or high interest rates, or the potential coordination of different policies for the ecological transition. This is structural coordination, which may involve setting common objectives.

There is also a need for cyclical coordination to prevent fiscal policy and monetary policy from having opposing effects on the economic cycle. It is easy to see the futility of a monetary policy that seeks to combat deflation by buying up Treasury bonds on a massive scale while fiscal policy is very restrictive at the same time.

Anti-inflation policies—especially when driven by energy prices—can only be effective if monetary policy is consistent with energy policy and various price control measures (as many European countries have imposed on gas or electricity prices, for example). Governments and central banks would benefit from making more formal joint commitments on economic trajectories and how the mix between fiscal and monetary policy can contribute to these objectives.

One way of formalizing the coordination between these two policies in Europe would be to include the central bank in the "European Semester" process (i.e., the system for coordinating the economic and budgetary policies of EU member states). This six-month period, which aims to synchronize national policies, begins with a series of reports from the European Commission, one of which consists of recommendations for the direction of budgetary policy in the EU and its member states over the course of the year. On this occasion, the ECB could announce how it intends to coordinate its policy with that of the EU (or oppose it, if it believes that its mandate and independence justify going in the opposite direction to that recommended by the Commission).

"HELICOPTER MONEY"

A radical example of coordination between monetary policy and fiscal policy might be what economists call "helicopter money." For the central bank, that is a direct transfer of money to citizens in order to avoid a major economic crisis that would cause prices and employment to decrease. It is an exceptional and short-term monetary policy measure whose objectives and means are distinct but close to those of a temporary fiscal stimulus. In practice, this policy would be similar to sending a check to every adult, as the government of the United States did during the COVID-19 pandemic in the name of economic stimulus. Contrary to what is possible in Europe, in the United States the central bank is not authorized to make payments to individuals. Nonetheless, the form could be different: rather than a check, it might take the form of a prepaid card, or citizens' (hypothetical) accounts at the central bank might be credited directly.[40]

If the central bank aims to maintain price stability, and if it has announced that its inflation target is close to 2 percent, it would be justified in using any instrument in its power to achieve this objective in the case of a period of low but prolonged inflation, as was the case, for example, in the eurozone between 2015 and 2020. If the central bank and the state share the same diagnosis of the economy, the only remaining question is whether the central bank or the government should set up this monetary transfer to households.

In this case, as always, coordination is necessary. And there are good reasons for thinking that it is up to the central bank to act. First, it would be less costly politically for the central bank to put an end to this transfer once its objective is achieved. Second, it would be more transparent democratically for the central bank to make transfers directly to households than to buy public debt in order to allow the government to make the payments as a second step. Third, this new tool of monetary policy can reduce the dependency of the banks on the central bank and thus diminish the side effects of central bank asset purchases on wealth inequality and financial instability. Last, making monetary policy without passing through loans to banks may include the advantage of "democratizing" the debate on monetary policy by making the central bank's action more tangible for individuals.

Two arguments are generally advanced against the kind of monetary policy in which direct transfers of money are made to households. These criticisms are not specific to the action of the central bank; they are framed in the same way if a check sent by the government is involved. The first is the question of redistribution and equity: Is it legitimate to give everyone the same amount? This question is in part resolved by the progressiveness of the fiscal system: since there is no reason why this monetary transfer should not be taxed as revenue, it will be subjected to the progressive tax. After taxes, the wealthiest citizens will therefore receive less.

The second objection is more fundamental: Is it necessary to jump-start growth through consumption, no matter the price? Instead, shouldn't we be glad about weak inflation and growth, at least from the point of view of the environment? So long as our societies have not resolved the problem of unemployment and the reconciliation of zero growth with full employment, monetary policy must retain the objective of moderate inflation and full employment. But it is also true that the imperative of controlled inflation can no longer be disconnected from environmental concerns.

INFLATION AND THE ENVIRONMENT

The changes required to modify our relationship to growth and employment greatly exceed the current framework of monetary policy. As we have seen, the role of monetary policy in this context is to create the optimal conditions for financing ecological investments and to take into account the connections between climate risk and economic and financial risks. But it is also essential that the central banks prepare themselves for a world in which consumption and the growth of GDP would no longer be the principal indicators of macroeconomic policy and would instead make room for measures of environmental sustainability and well-being.[41]

Paradoxically, it is also possible that in such a world, the objective of price stability might remain more pertinent than the growth of the GDP, even though the definition of the price index may need to be adapted. The price index has two characteristics that make it particularly adaptable to the ecological transition. First, it is an index weighted in accord with consumption. If the state discourages the consumption of a particularly polluting good by taxing it heavily, the price index will increase little if this good is actually not much consumed. Second, the price index is calculated at constant quality. In other words, the national statistical institutes examine the development of the prices of a given good while taking into account the development of its quality. If the environmental quality is included in this calculation, then the price of goods whose environmental quality deteriorates will rise, whereas the price of goods whose quality improves will stabilize. This is not limited to climate sustainability and can be extended to the improvement of biodiversity.

These simple arguments have important consequences for monetary policy. In the ideal scenario of ecological transition, the prices for carbon-based energies increase, followed by a decrease in their consumption and their replacement by sources of energy that are more respectful of the environment. Thus, carbon-based energies are consumed less after the increase in their price, and their weight in the consumer price index consequently declines. The rise in the price of carbon would therefore not lead to a rise in the rate of inflation. But if this substitution takes time—and the first months of the war in Ukraine demonstrated this—and the increases in the prices of energy are passed on in the prices of other goods (food, services, etc.), then the central bank would face a delicate situation. Reducing the rate of inflation might conflict with the objective of protecting the environment. A radical solution would be for the central bank to decide to target a rate of inflation in which the proportions of the different kinds of energy consumed reflect environmental objectives and not the reality of consumption. But would such a solution be accepted politically?

As this example illustrates, we have entered a world in which monetary policy must be coordinated with an energy and environmental policy that seeks to immediately replace carbon-based energies with sources that are not based on carbon. Without this coordination, contradictions between environmental goals and price stability will become problematic. Or inversely, it might be that the ecological transition requires a change in the relationship between consumer prices and unemployment. There is currently a great deal of uncertainty regarding this question. If the state does not have an employment policy adapted to the ecological transition—increasing the employment rate despite a drop in production—then the central bank might find itself pursuing an expansionary monetary policy in a climate of low inflation, in opposition to objectives of moderate consumption compatible with the environmental objectives.

The environmental question creates new dilemmas for monetary policy and will undoubtedly lead to a new way of thinking about and measuring macroeconomic goals. But the question arises: In a democratic society, who should make decisions regarding such changes and, above all, how?

The Central Bank Belongs to Democracy

The crisis of 2008–2009 marked a turning point in the history of central banks. History does not move forward by turning back; it is better to assess and measure an upheaval than to cultivate nostalgia for a bygone era. And the current upheaval is not without foundation. We can understand the evolution of monetary policy over the past fifteen years not only as the fulfillment of the essential role that the central bank plays in the welfare state, but also as the fulfillment of its role as the conductor of the financial system as a whole. This dual—and often contradictory—role is the product of a long history.

The democratic framework in which central banks have evolved must be rethought in order to account for the financial and political importance they have taken on and the new forms of their intervention in the economic system. This imperative is all the more important as the central bank's actions necessarily impact the pricing of public debt and the ecological transition, as well as the function and scope of digital currency.

The *democratic reappropriation* advocated in this book is not about making central banks part of the elected government, as purely procedural conceptions of democracy that are limited to matters of elections and parliamentary representation would have it. While the government plays an essential role in democracy, a democracy must also live outside the government by institutionalizing deliberation and checks and balances in the functions of its administrative authorities, including the central bank.

Another lesson of this book is that we should never conceive of the role of a central bank in isolation. Too many debates on monetary policy meet dead ends because they remove the central bank from its context, ignoring the links between monetary and credit policies as well as the complex and multilateral relations that the central bank maintains with the public treasury, private banks, and public investment banks.

The policies of the central banks obviously have effects on financial actors, but historically it is the central banks that have adapted to the changes in the banking and financial sectors (including those caused by political reforms or crises), much more often than the other way around. We must therefore think at the level of the financial system and, from there, imagine the role of credit policy and the central bank within it.

These reflections on the legitimacy of the central bank, including the scope of its financial operations or the possible issuance of a new digital currency, converge with other, fundamental questions. These are questions of economic policy, of the justification and efficacy of state intervention, of the degree of independence and parliamentary oversight of the administrative authorities. Here, and elsewhere, it is important to remember that the making of monetary policy is not autonomous, nor is it isolated from the classic problems of economic policy—or democracy, for that matter.

As is the case for any democratic institution, the law alone does not guarantee the legitimacy of the central bank. The central bank is to be judged on the basis of its acts and justifications, and therefore on the basis of its ability to insure the public utility of the currency. That is how the public support that is the source of the central bank's power can live on.

Notes

1. Pierre Rosanvallon, *Democratic Legitimacy: Impartiality, Reflexivity, Proximity* (Princeton, NJ: Princeton University Press, 2013); Antoine Vauchez, *Democratizing Europe* (New York: Palgrave MacMillan, 2016).

2. Even the conservative Montagu Norman, governor of the Bank of England and a supporter of the gold standard during the interwar period, pointed out that the independence of a central bank—which he considered an absolute principle—implied a "close and continuous cooperation between the bank and the government when important issues are involved." See preface to Cecil H. Kisch and W. T. A. Elkin, *Central Banks: A Study of the Constitutions of Banks of Issue, with an Analysis of Representative Charters* (London; Macmillan, 1932; New York: Garland, 1983), 8.

3. This approach merges with the one Lev Menand developed regarding the United States, *The Fed Unbound: Central Banking in a Time of Crisis* (New York: Columbia Global Reports, 2022).

1. The "euthanasia of the rentier," an expression that Maynard Keynes uses to describe the consequences of inflation, is connected with the fact that the real value of capital decreases along with a rise in prices. In the course of history, public and private debts have been reduced by inflation. But this negative effect on the wealthiest individuals makes itself felt chiefly in the medium term, whereas the effect on the poorest is immediate. Thus the redistributive effects of inflation result from a complex set of phenomena over which the central bank itself has little control.

2. The choice of a floating exchange rate is also always made by the government, even in countries where the central bank is legally very independent, as it is in the euro-

zone: the choice of the exchange policy is made by the Council of the European Union and not by the central bank (Treaty on the Functioning of the European Union, art. 219).

3. Credit is the operation through which money is lent to someone else. But that does not mean that currency in the form of savings necessarily precedes credit, as the customary saying *les crédits font les dépôts* ("loans make deposits") suggests.

4. Victor Degorce and Éric Monnet, "The Great Depression as a Saving Glut," Centre for Economic Policy Research Discussion Paper 15287 (September 12, 2020).

5. On the preceding period, see Ulrich Bindseil, *Central Banking before 1800: A Rehabilitation* (New York: Oxford University Press, 2019). Chapter 3 of the present book will return to the important exception of the United States in the course of the nineteenth century.

6. Degorce and Monnet, "The Great Depression."

7. The alternative proposal formulated at the time was to force commercial banks to deposit in the central bank an amount equivalent to the deposits of individuals that they received (i.e., 100 percent reserves). Thus, the goal was to disconnect the system of lending from sovereign monetary creation. On this history, see Ronnie J. Phillips, *The Chicago Plan and New Deal Banking Reform* (New York: Routledge, 2016).

8. On this history and its consequences for the 2008–2009 crisis, see especially Adam Tooze, *Crashed: How a Decade of Financial Crises Changed the World* (New York: Viking, 2018), chaps. 2 and 6; Matthias Thiemann, *The Growth of Shadow Banking: A Comparative Institutional Analysis* (Cambridge: Cambridge University Press, 2018).

9. For the French case, see Éric Monnet, *Controlling Credit: Central Banking and the Planned Economy in Postwar France, 1948–1973* (Cambridge: Cambridge University Press, 2018), chap. 5. This was also the case for the United States before 1981. See Kenneth D. Garbade, *After the Accord: A History of Federal Reserve Open Market Operations, the US Government Securities Market, and Treasury Debt Management from 1951 to 1979* (Cambridge: Cambridge University Press, 2021); William Bateman, "The Fiscal Fed" (paper presented at Central Banking and Its Discontents Conference, Heinrich Böll Foundation, Berlin, July 11–13, 2022).

10. Gary Gorton, "The History and Economics of Safe Assets," *Annual Review of Economics* 9 (2017): 547–86; Eric Monnet, "Why Central Bankers Should Read Economic History," *Books and Ideas* [Collège de France], February 8, 2021; Daniela Gabor, "Revolution without Revolutionaries: Interrogating the Return of Monetary Financing," *SocArXiv*, March 11, 2021, https://doi.org/10.31235/osf.io/ja9bk.

11. Eric Monnet and Blaise Truong-Loï, "The History and Politics of Public Debt Accounting," in *A World of Public Debts: A Political History*, ed. N. Barreyre and N. Delalande (Cham: Palgrave Macmillan, 2020), 481–511.

12. Daniela Gabor, "The (Impossible) Repo Trinity: The Political Economy of Repo Markets," *Review of International Political Economy* 23, no. 6 (2016): 967–1000.

13. Recall that up to the beginning of the twentieth century, the central banks were essentially European institutions. At that time, Japan was the only non-European country that had one, established in 1897. The United States followed suit in 1913.

14. Miroslav A. Kriz, "Central Banks and the State Today," *American Economic Review* 38, no. 4 (1948): 565–80.

15. Kriz.

16. Tim Sablik, "Fed Credit Policy during the Great Depression," Federal Reserve Bank of Richmond Economic Brief 13-03 (March 2013).

17. Greta R. Krippner, "The Making of US Monetary Policy: Central Bank Transparency and the Neoliberal Dilemma," *Theory and Society* 36 (2007): 477–513.

18. See, for example, in the US debate, Henry C. Simons, "Rules versus Authorities in Monetary Policy," *Journal of Political Economy* 44, no. 1 (1936): 1–30. To judge the extent to which the dominant liberal view of the 1900s differs from that of the 1930s, see Stanley Fischer, "Rules versus Discretion in Monetary Policy," *Handbook of Monetary Economics* 2 (1990): 1155–84.

19. Barry Eichengreen, *Hall of Mirrors: The Great Depression, the Great Recession, and the Uses and Misuses of History* (Oxford: Oxford University Press, 2014); Patrice Baubeau, Éric Monnet, Angelo Riva, and Stefano Ungaro, "Flight-to-Safety and the Credit Crunch: A New History of the Banking Crises in France during the Great Depression," *Economic History Review* 74, no. 1 (2021): 223–50.

20. That is not legally incompatible with the fact that the ECB has to operate "in conformity with the principle of an open-market economy in which competition is free, promoting an efficient allocation of resources." Treaty Establishing the European Community, part 3, title 7, chapter 2, article 105. See chapter 5.

21. Gøsta Esping-Andersen, *The Three Worlds of Welfare Capitalism* (Princeton, NJ: Princeton University Press, 1990).

22. A whole new field, where research is very active in sociology and political science, emphasizes this point in the current context. See, among others, Peter Dietsch, François Claveau, and Clément Fontan, *Do Central Banks Serve the People?* (Cambridge: Polity, 2018); Benjamin Braun and Daniela Gabor, "Central Banking, Shadow Banking, and Infrastructural Power," *SocArXiv*, March 13, 2019, https://doi.org/10.31235/osf.io/nf9ms.

23. Karl Polanyi, *The Great Transformation: The Political and Economic Origins of Our Time* (New York: Farrar and Rinehart, 1944; Boston: Beacon Press, 2001), 201.

24. Charles Goodhart, *The Evolution of Central Banks* (Cambridge, MA: MIT Press 1988), 7. The phenomenon of moral hazards that Goodhart describes does not concern only each financial institution in isolation. We can use the term "collective moral hazard" to describe the fact that commercial banks anticipate having access to the central banks' liquidity and thus take greater risks. See Emmanuel Farhi and Jean Tirole, "Col-

lective Moral Hazard, Maturity Mismatch, and Systemic Bailouts," *American Economic Review* 102, no. 1 (2012): 60–93.

25. Monnet, *Controlling Credit*, chaps. 3 and 7.

26. The governor of the Bank of England, Mervyn King, was in favor of returning to this kind of system. King, *The End of Alchemy: Money, Banking, and the Future of the Global Economy* (New York: W. W. Norton, 2016). Although open-market purchases and sales of assets have become the main instruments of monetary policy implementation, central banks still offer standing facilities to credit institutions (e.g., a "marginal lending facility" and a "deposit facility" in the Eurosystem, as well as "discount window lending" and a "standing repo facility" in the US Federal Reserve).

27. Robert McCauley, "The Federal Reserve Needs the Power to Buy Corporate Bonds," *VoxEu.org*, August 26, 2020.

28. Perry Mehrling, *The New Lombard Street: How the Fed Became the Dealer of Last Resort* (Princeton, NJ: Princeton University Press, 2010).

29. Guillaume Bazot, "Local Liquidity Constraints: What Place for Central Bank Regional Policy?," *Explorations in Economic History* 52 (2014): 44–62; Jane Ellen Knodell, *The Second Bank of the United States: "Central" Banker in an Era of Nation-Building, 1816–1836* (London: Taylor & Francis, 2017); Stefano Ugolini, *The Evolution of Central Banking: Theory and History* (London: Palgrave Macmillan, 2017).

30. Guillaume Bazot, Eric Monnet, and Matthias Morys, "Taming the Global Financial Cycle: Central Banks as Shock Absorbers in the First Era of Globalization," *Journal of Economic History* 82, no. 3 (2022): 801–39.

31. Lawrence J. Broz, *The International Origins of the Federal Reserve System* (Ithaca, NY: Cornell University Press, 1997).

32. Adam Smith, *The Wealth of Nations* (New York: Random House, 1994), bk. 2, chap. 2, 348.

33. Stephany Griffith-Jones and José Antonio Ocampo, eds., *The Future of National Development Banks* (Oxford: Oxford University Press, 2018); Daniel Mertens, Matthias Thiemann, and Peter Volberding, eds., *The Reinvention of Development Banking in the European Union* (New York: Oxford University Press, 2021); Thomas Marois, *Public Banks: Decarbonisation, Definancialisation and Democratisation* (Cambridge: Cambridge University Press, 2021).

34. Through a special program called pledged supplementary lending, the Public Bank of China refinances on favorable terms the two great Chinese development banks (the China Development Bank, the Agricultural Development Bank of China) and the bank that finances foreign trade (the Export-Import Bank of China).

35. On the dual nature of liquidity (precaution versus speculation) and its importance in the history of financial capitalism, see Jon Levy, *Ages of American Capitalism: A History of the United States* (New York: Random House, 2021).

CHAPTER TWO

1. The guarantee can be a financial security or a loan granted by the bank. If the bank does not repay the loan, the central bank can therefore keep the security and resell it, or else demand the money and lend it to the borrower to which the bank originally granted the loan.

2. Historically, it has been possible to limit central banks' ability to create money by means of two kinds of laws: either a ceiling on the number of bills printed, or (in gold-standard or silver-standard countries) by a ratio between money and bank deposits (liabilities) and international assets. Gold and silver were considered international assets.

3. On these complex phenomena, see Garreth Rule, "Understanding the Central Bank Balance Sheet," Bank of England, Centre for Central Banking Studies Publication Series 32 (December 2015).

4. Alan Taylor, *The Great Leveraging*, Centre for Economic Policy Research Discussion Paper 9082 (July 2012).

5. Michael Magill, Martine Quinzii, and Jean-Charles Rochet, "The Safe Asset, Banking Equilibrium, and Optimal Central Bank Monetary, Prudential, and Balance-Sheet Policies," *Journal of Monetary Economics* 112, no. 1 (2020): 113–28.

6. Thomas Piketty, *Le capital au XXIe siècle* (Paris: Seuil, 2013).

7. Niall Ferguson, Andreas Schaab, and Moritz Schularick, "Central Bank Balance Sheets: Expansion and Reduction since 1900," Centre for Economic Policy Research Discussion Paper 10635 (June 1, 2015).

8. Ugo Albertazzi, Bo Becker, and Miguel Boucinha, "Portfolio Rebalancing and the Transmission of Large-Scale Asset Purchase Programs: Evidence from the Euro Area," *Journal of Financial Intermediation* 48 (October 2020): 100896; Itay Goldstein, Jonathan Witmer, and Jing Yang, "Following the Money: Evidence for the Portfolio Balance Channel of Quantitative Easing," Bank of Canada Staff Working Paper 2018-33 (July 2018).

9. Ulrich Bindseil and Luc Laeven, "Confusion about the Lender of Last Resort," *VoxEU.org*, January 13, 2017.

10. Sebastian Grund, Nele Nomm, and Florian Walch, "Liquidity in Resolution: Comparing Frameworks for Liquidity Provision across Jurisdictions," European Central Bank Occasional Paper 2020-251 (December 2020).

11. Among the few central banks that have private shareholders, the shareholders have no control over decisions, and the dividends are monitored. In the United States, the regional Federal Reserve Banks have private shareholders. Bernd Bartels, Beatrice Weder di Mauro, and Barry Eichengreen, "No Smoking Gun: Private Shareholders, Governance Rules and Central Bank Financial Behavior," Centre for Economic Policy Research Discussion Paper 168251 (2016).

12. For a discussion of the Swiss case, which deals with both recapitalization by the

government in the 1970s and the aversion to losses, see, for example, Thomas Jordan, "Does the Swiss National Bank Need Equity?" (lecture, Statistisch-Volkswirtschaftliche Gesellschaft Basel, September 28, 2011).

13. Ricardo Reis, "Central Bank Design," *Journal of Economic Perspectives* 27, no. 4 (2013): 17–44. That is what the Banque de France did during World War I. See Éric Monnet and Vincent Duchaussoy, "La Banque de France et le financement du Trésor pendant la Première Guerre mondiale," in *La mobilisation financière pendant la Grande Guerre*, ed. Florence Descamps and Laure Quennouëlle-Corre (Paris: CHEFF, 2015), 121–52.

14. Fabian Amtenbrink, "Securing Financial Independence in the Legal Basis of a Central Bank," in *The Capital Needs of Central Banks*, ed. Sue Milton and Peter Sinclair (New York: Routledge, 2010), 83–95.

15. On the recent legal issues surrounding government transfers to the central banks, see Will Bateman, "The Law of Monetary Finance under Unconventional Monetary Policy," *Oxford Journal of Legal Studies* 41, no. 4 (2021): 929–64.

16. Alain Naef and Jens van 't Klooster, "Responsibility for Emissions: The Case of the Swiss National Bank's Foreign Exchange Reserves and the Norwegian Oil Fund," Banque de France Working Paper 872 (2022).

17. For a recent well-articulated defense of this point of view, see Jesús Fernández-Villaverde, Daniel Sanches, Linda Schilling, and Harald Uhlig, "Central Bank Digital Currency: Central Banking for All?," *Review of Economic Dynamics* 41 (July 2021): 225–42.

CHAPTER THREE

1. Éric Monnet, *Controlling Credit: Central Banking and the Planned Economy in Postwar France, 1948–1973* (Cambridge: Cambridge University Press, 2018), chap.7.

2. Benjamin Friedman, "The Future of Monetary Policy: The Central Bank as an Army with Only a Signal Corps?," *International Finance* 2, no. 3 (1999): 321–38.

3. Will Bateman, "The Law of Monetary Finance under Unconventional Monetary Policy," *Oxford Journal of Legal Studies* 41, no. 4 (2021): 929–64.

4. Similar rules existed in most European countries (see Monnet, *Controlling Credit*) and in the United States (see Kenneth D. Garbade, *After the Accord: A History of Federal Reserve Open Market Operations, the US Government Securities Market, and Treasury Debt Management from 1951 to 1979* [Cambridge: Cambridge University Press, 2021]).

5. For a complete and detailed account of these events, see Adam Tooze, *Crashed: Comment une décennie de crise financière a changé le monde* (Paris: Les Belles Lettres, 2018).

6. European Parliament, "Résolution du Parlement européen du 13 mars 2014 sur le rapport d'enquête sur le rôle et les activités de la troïka [the ECB, European Com-

mission, and IMF] dans les pays sous-programme de la zone euro," *europarl.europa.eu*, March 13, 2014.

7. Peter Gauweiler and Others v. Deutscher Bundestag, case C-62/15, European Union Court of Justice (grande chambre), ruling of June 16, 2015.

8. More precisely, each country's share of the ECB's capital ("clé de capital"), which is a function of the population and the GDP of the various countries.

9. See the analysis and the context of this report in Monnet, *Controlling Credit*, 251.

10. Jens van 't Klooster and Rens van Tilburg, "Targeting a Sustainable Recovery with Green TLTROs," *SocArXiv*, December 18, 2020, http://doi.org/10.31235/osf.io/2bx8h.

11. Eric Lonergan and Megan Greene, "Dual Interest Rates Give Central Banks Limitless Firepower," *VoxEU.org*, September 20, 2020.

12. Technically, it created and loaned to a distinct financial institution (Maiden Lane) that had been assigned to liquidate these bankrupt institutions.

13. Tooze, *Crashed*, chap. 9; Perry Mehrling, "Elasticity and Discipline in the Global Swap Network," *International Journal of Political Economy* 44, no. 4 (2015): 311–24.

14. Iñaki Aldasoro, Torsten Ehlers, Patrick McGuire, and Goetz von Peter, "Global Banks' Dollar Funding Needs and Central Bank Swap Lines," *BIS Bulletin* no. 27 (2020).

15. Daniela Gabor and Shahin Vallée, "Three Ideas to Improve the International Role of the ECB," DGAP commentary no. 4 (February 11, 2021); Lukas Spielberger, "The Politicisation of the European Central Bank and Its Emergency Credit Lines outside the Euro Area," *Journal of European Public Policy* 30, no. 5 (2022): 873–97.

16. Guillaume Bazot, Michael D. Bordo, and Éric Monnet, "International Shocks and the Balance Sheet of the Bank of France under the Classical Gold Standard," *Explorations in Economic History* 62 (2016): 87–107.

17. Barry Eichengreen et al., "Is Capital Account Convertibility Required for the Renminbi to Acquire Reserve Currency Status?," CEPR Press Discussion Paper 17498 (2022).

18. Michael Perks, Yudong Rao, Jongsoon Shin, and Kiichi Tokuoka, "Evolution of Bilateral Swap Lines," IMF Working Paper 2021/210 (2021).

19. In parallel, China has become the world's primary creditor, with direct loans made to states and enterprises. Sebastian Horn, Carmen M. Reinhart, and Christoph Trebesch, "China's Overseas Lending," *Journal of International Economics* 133 (2021): 103539.

20. Lukas Spielberger, "The Politicisation of the European Central Bank and Its Emergency Credit Lines Outside the Euro Area," *Journal of European Public Policy* 30, no. 5 (2022): 1–25.

21. Alexander R. Perry, "The Federal Reserve's Questionable Legal Basis for Foreign Central Bank Liquidity Swaps," *Columbia Law Review* 120, no. 3 (2020): 729–68.

22. Anton Korinek, "The New Economics of Prudential Capital Controls: A Research Agenda," *IMF Economic Review*, 59, no. 3 (2011): 523–61; Rafaël Cezar and Eric Monnet,

"Capital Controls and Foreign Reserves against External Shocks: Combined or Alone?," Banque de France document de travail 849 (2021).

23. Evgenia Passari and Hélène Rey, "Financial Flows and the International Monetary System," *Economic Journal* 125, no. 584 (2015): 675–98.

24. Barry Eichengreen and Andrew Rose, "Capital Controls in the Twenty-First Century," *Journal of International Money and Finance* 48 (2014): 1–16.

25. The IMF's senior economists overtly criticized the inadequacy of this position. Anton Korinek, Prakash Loungani, and Jonathan D. Ostry, "The IMF's Updated View on Capital Controls: Welcome Fixes but Major Rethinking Is Still Needed," *Brookings*, April 18, 2022.

26. Eichengreen et al., "Is Capital Account Convertibility Required for the Renminbi to Acquire Reserve Currency Status?"

27. Marc Schwartz and Yannis Messaoui, "Le grand paradoxe—ou pourquoi le règne du cash est loin de s'achever," *Terra Nova*, January 8, 2021; Brett Scott, *Cloudmoney: Cash, Cards, Crypto, and the War for Our Wallets* (New York: Harper Business, 2022).

28. One hypothesis would be that coins and bills might be reserved for local currencies whose use still remains marginal today. See Jérôme Blanc, *Les monnaies alternatives* (Paris: La Découverte, 2019).

29. Raphael Auer et al., "Central Bank Digital Currencies: Motives, Economic Implications, and the Research Frontier," *Annual Review of Economics* 14 (2022): 697–721.

30. In France, as in Europe, liquid deposits represent about 20 percent of the banks' total liabilities. If we attempt to make a more accurate estimate by limiting this sum to deposits made by residents, using French data (in particular, regulated liquid savings, such as tax-exempt savings accounts like the "livret A" or a sustainable development savings book), the share of liquid deposits does not exceed 10 percent.

31. Ulrich Bindseil, "Tiered CBDC and the Financial System" European Central Bank Discussion Paper 2351 (2020); Eric Monnet, Angelo Riva, and Stefano Ungaro, "The Real Effects of Bank Runs: Evidence from the French Great Depression (1930–1931)," CEPR Discussion Paper 16054 (2021).

32. Michael D. Bordo, "Central Bank Digital Currency in Historical Perspective: Another Crossroad in Monetary History," NBER Working Paper 29171 (2021).

CHAPTER FOUR

1. For a comparative approach to central banks during these two periods, see Pierre Siklos, *The Changing Face of Central Banking: Evolutionary Trends since World War II* (Cambridge: Cambridge University Press, 2002); Guillaume Bazot, Éric Monnet, and≈Matthias Morys, "Taming the Global Financial Cycle: Central Banks as Shock Absorbers in the First Era of Globalization," *Journal of Economic History* 82, no. 3 (2022): 801–39.

2. Claudio Borio, "The Implementation of Monetary Policy in Industrial Countries: A Survey," BIS Economic Papers, no. 47 (1997); Dieter Gerdesmeier, Francesco Paolo Mongelli, and Barbara Roffia, "The Eurosystem, the US Federal Reserve, and the Bank of Japan: Similarities and Differences," *Journal of Money, Credit and Banking* 39, no. 7 (2007): 1785–19.

3. Andrew Shonfield, *Modern Capitalism. The Changing Balance of Public and Private Power* (Oxford: Oxford University Press, 1960); Bruno Amable, *The Diversity of Modern Capitalism* (Oxford: Oxford University Press, 2003).

4. Network for Greening the Financial System, "First Progress Report," November 10, 2018.

5. This is also the case in the eurozone, where the status of the ESCB has a constitutional value, because it is written into the founding treaties of the European Union.

6. Central Bank Governance Group, *Issues in the Governance of Central Banks* (Basel: Bank for International Settlements, 2009).

7. Rosa María Lastra, "The Institutional Path of Central Bank Independence," in *Research Handbook on Central Banking*, ed. Peter Conti-Brown and Rosa María Lastra (Northampton, MA: Edward Elgar, 2018): 296–313.

8. According to the most reliable recent study in this field, the central bank of China is supposed to be much more independent than, for example, the central banks of the United Kingdom or Australia. See Davide Romelli, "The Political Economy of Reforms in Central Bank Design: Evidence from a New Dataset," *Economic Policy* (2022): eiac011. This incongruity is explained by the fact that the measure of central banks' independence is founded only on legal texts that, in this case, give a larger role to British parliaments and governments in determining the central banks' objectives. In practice, however, there is no doubt that China's central bank is less autonomous with respect to the government than the other central banks mentioned earlier. It makes no attempt to conceal this, since its website states that it applies literally the instructions of the Central Committee of the Chinese communist party and the State Council of the People's Republic of China.

9. Bateman, "The Law of Monetary Finance under Unconventional Monetary Policy."

10. I expressed my opposition to such a proposal of cancellation, which in my view would have limited the ECB's future ability to buy public debt and to strengthen the link between budgetary rules and monetary policy. Benjamin Lemoine, Éric Monnet, and Benjamin Braun, "Beware the Low-Hanging Fruit," *IPS*, March 3, 2021, https://www.ips-journal.eu/topics/european-integration/beware-the-low-hanging-fruit-5019/.

11. Christopher Adolph, *Bankers, Bureaucrats, and Central Bank Politics: The Myth of Neutrality* (Cambridge: Cambridge University Press, 2013); Christopher Adolph, "The Missing Politics of Central Banks," *PS: Political Science & Politics* 51, no. 4 (2018):

737–42. Economic theories rarely take into account the pressures that are exercised on the central banks by both governments and private interest groups. An exception is Emmanuelle Gabillon and David Martimort, "The Benefits of Central Bank's Political Independence," *European Economic Review* 48, no. 2 (2004): 353–78.

12. Eric Monnet and Damien Puy, "Do Old Habits Die Hard? Central Banks and the Bretton Woods Gold Puzzle," *Journal of International Economics* 127 (2020): 103394.

13. Lastra, "The Institutional Path of Central Bank Independence."

14. Peter Conti-Brown, *The Power and Independence of the Federal Reserve* (Princeton, NJ: Princeton University Press, 2017).

15. For a critique of this system (and of the argument according to which it contributes to the diversity of points of view), see Conti-Brown, chap. 11.

16. Benoît Cœuré, "Heterogeneity and the European Central Bank's Monetary Policy" (speech at the Bank of France Symposium and 34th SUERF Colloquium "The Euro Area: Staying the Course through Uncertainties," Paris, March 29, 2019).

17. See Guillaume Bazot, Eric Monnet, and Matthias Morys, "The Flexibility of the Classical Gold Standard (1870s–1914): Any Lessons for the Eurozone?," in *The Economics of Monetary Unions*, ed. Juan Castaneda (London: Routledge, 2020): 17–30.

18. In the United States, a similar system between regional central banks existed until 1975, even after the creation of the Federal Open Market Committee in 1933. Today, transfers between banks are balanced each year, but they are for small amounts.

19. The dollar represents 60 percent of worldwide foreign exchange reserves; the euro, 20 percent.

20. This situation is called a currency board. Argentina was in this situation with regard to the dollar from 1991 to 2002. Among other examples, today Bulgaria and Bosnia have a currency board pegged to the euro.

21. Ethan Ilzetzki, Carmen M. Reinhart, and Kenneth S. Rogoff, "Exchange Arrangements Entering the Twenty-First Century: Which Anchor Will Hold?," *Quarterly Journal of Economics* 134, no. 2 (2019): 599–646.

22. Manuela Moschella, "Currency Wars in the Advanced World: Resisting Appreciation at a Time of Change in Central Banking Monetary Consensus," *Review of International Political Economy* 22, no. 1 (2015): 134–61.

23. Alain Naef and Jens van 't Klooster, "Responsibility for Emissions: The Case of the Swiss National Bank's Foreign Exchange Reserves and the Norwegian Oil Fund," Banque de France Working Paper 872 (2022).

24. Charles Goodhart and Dirk Schoenmaker, "Should the Functions of Monetary Policy and Banking Supervision Be Separated?," *Oxford Economic Papers* 47, no. 4 (1995): 539–60.

25. Donato Masciandaro and Marc Quintyn, "The Governance of Financial Supervision: Recent Developments," *Journal of Economic Surveys* 30 no. 5 (2016): 982–1006.

26. Éric Monnet, *Controlling Credit: Central Banking and the Planned Economy in Postwar France, 1948–1973* (Cambridge: Cambridge University Press, 2018).

27. Grund, Nomm, and Walch, "Liquidity in Resolution."

28. In Europe, all these formats exist. See European Banking Authority, Consumer Corner, https://www.eba.europa.eu/consumer-corner/national-competent-authorities -for-consumer-protection, Particularly because of the multiplicity of models, the financial protection of consumers is not centralized by the ECB in the European Union.

29. Conti-Brown, *The Power and Independence of the Federal Reserve*, 191–292.

30. Erlend Nier et al., "Institutional Models for Macroprudential Policy," IMF Staff Discussion Note SDN/11/18 (November 1, 2011).

31. David Aikman et al., "Would Macroprudential Regulation Have Prevented the Last Crisis?," *Journal of Economic Perspectives* 33, no. 1 (2019): 107–30. See also Lev Menand, *The Fed Unbound: Central Banking in a Time of Crisis* (New York: Columbia Global Reports, 2022), chap. 4, on the danger represented by money market funds.

32. Domenico Lombardi and Manuela Moschella, "The Symbolic Politics of Delegation: Macroprudential Policy and Independent Regulatory Authorities," *New Political Economy* 22, no. 1 (2017): 92–108.

33. European Central Bank/European Systemic Risk Board, Project Team on Climate Risk Monitoring, "The Macroprudential Challenge of Climate Change," July 2022.

34. Éric Monnet and Miklos Vari, "A Dilemma between Liquidity Regulation and Monetary Policy: Some History and Theory," *Journal of Money, Credit and Banking* 55, no. 4 (2022): 915–44.

35. On this history, see Monnet, *Controlling Credit*, chap.7.

36. Milton Friedman, *The Optimum Quantity of Money and Other Essays* (Chicago: Aldine, 1969), 75; Marvin Goodfriend, "Why We Need an 'Accord' for Federal Reserve Credit Policy: A Note," *Journal of Money, Credit and Banking* 26, no. 3 (1994): 572–80. While Goodfriend is critical of the Fed's credit policy and wants to manage it, he recognizes its existence and does not advocate an abandonment of the term.

37. Adrien Auclert, "Monetary Policy and the Redistribution Channel," *American Economic Review* 109, no. 6 (2019): 2333–67.

38. Karamfil Todorov, "Quantify the Quantitative Easing: Impact on Bonds and Corporate Debt Issuance," *Journal of Financial Economics* 135, no. 2 (2020): 340–58.

39. Ben Charoenwong, Randall Morck, and Yupana Wiwattanakantang, "Bank of Japan Equity Purchases: The (Non-)Effects of Extreme Quantitative Easing," *Review of Finance* 25, no. 3 (2021): 713–43.

40. Tim Sablik, "Fed Credit Policy during the Great Depression," Federal Reserve Bank of Richmond Economic Brief 13-03 (March 2013); Peter Conti-Brown, "Explaining the New Fed-Treasury Emergency Fund," Brookings Institution, April 3, 2020, https:// perma.cc/R9FQ-29LS.

41. Eric Milstein and David Wessel, "What Did the Fed Do in Response to the COVID-19 Crisis?," Brookings Institution, Hutchins Center on Fiscal and Monetary Policy, December 17, 2021.

42. Elsa Clara Massoc, "Having Banks 'Play Along': State-Bank Coordination and State-Guaranteed Credit Programs during the COVID-19 Crisis in France and Germany," *Journal of European Public Policy* 29, no. 7 (2021): 1135–52. See Eurofound (European Foundation of the Improvement of Living and Working Conditions), *EU Policy Watch: Database of National-Level Policy Measures*, https://static.eurofound.europa.eu/covid19db/index.html.

43. Monnet, *Controlling Credit*.

44. Sarah L. Quinn, *American Bonds: How Credit Markets Shaped a Nation* (Princeton, NJ: Princeton University Press, 2019).

45. Deborah Lucas, "Credit Policy as Fiscal Policy," *Brookings Papers on Economic Activity* 2016.1 (2016): 1–57.

46. Andrew J. Fieldhouse, Karel Mertens, and Morten O. Ravn, "The Macroeconomic Effects of Government Asset Purchases: Evidence from Postwar U.S. Housing Credit Policy," *Quarterly Journal of Economics* 133, no. 3 (2018): 1503–60.

47. Éric Monnet, Stefano Pagliari, and Shahin Vallée, "Beyond Financial Repression and Regulatory Capture: The Recomposition of European Financial Ecosystems after the Crisis," LSE "Europe in Question," Discussion Paper 147 (September 30, 2019).

CHAPTER FIVE

1. Rudiger Dornbusch, *Keys to Prosperity: Free Markets, Sound Money, and a Bit of Luck* (Cambridge, MA: MIT Press, 2002), 15.

2. Joseph Stiglitz, "Central Banking in a Democratic Society," *De Economist* 146, no. 2 (1998): 199–226 (216–17).

3. Eric Monnet, "New Central Banking Calls for a European Credit Council," *VoxEu. org*, March 26, 2021.

4. Paul Tucker, *Unelected Power: The Quest for Legitimacy in Central Banking and the Regulatory State* (Princeton, NJ: Princeton University Press, 2019), 569.

5. John B. Taylor, *Policy Stability and Economic Growth: Lessons from the Great Recession* (Washington, DC: Institute of Economic Affairs, 2016).

6. Notably following the foundational article by Finn E. Kydland and Edward C. Prescott, "Rules Rather than Discretion: The Inconsistency of Optimal Plans," *Journal of Political Economy* 85, no. 3 (1977): 473–91.

7. Friedrich A. von Hayek, "The Constitution of a Liberal State," *Il Politico* 32, no. 3 (1967): 460.

8. Pierre Rosanvallon, *Democratic Legitimacy: Impartiality, Reflexivity, Proximity* (Princeton, NJ: Princeton University Press, 2013), 242–44.

9. Oliver Hart, "Incomplete Contracts and Control," *American Economic Review* 107, no. 7 (2017): 1731–52.

10. Chiara Zilioli and Antonio Luca Riso, "New Tasks and Central Bank Independence: The Eurosystem Experience," in *Research Handbook on Central Banking*, ed. Peter Conti-Brown and Rosa María Lastra (Northampton, MA: Edward Elgar, 2018), 155–83.

11. Luis Garicano and Rosa María Lastra, "Towards a New Architecture for Financial Stability: Seven Principles," *Journal of International Economic Law* 13, no. 3 (2010): 597–621; Jonathan Zeitlin and Filipe Brito Bastos, "SSM and the SRB Accountability at European Level: Room for Improvements?," European Parliament, Directorate-General for Internal Policies, Governance Support Unit (EGOV) (2020), https://www.europarl.europa.eu/thinktank/en/document/IPOL_IDA(2020)645747; Saule T. Omarova, "The 'Too Big to Fail' Problem," *Minnesota Law Review* 103 (2018): 2495–541.

12. Rosanvallon, *Democratic Legitimacy*, 238, 258.

13. Jens van 't Klooster, "The Ethics of Delegating Monetary Policy," *Journal of Politics* 82, no. 2 (2020): 587–99.

14. Thomas Christiano, "Rational Deliberation among Experts and Citizens," in *Deliberative Systems: Deliberative Democracy at the Large Scale*, ed. John Parkinson and Jane Mansbridge (New York: Cambridge University Press, 2012), 27–51; David Estlund and Hélène Landemore, "The Epistemic Value of Democratic Deliberation," in *The Oxford Handbook of Deliberative Democracy*, ed. André Bächtiger, John S. Dryzek, Jane Mansbridge, and Mark E. Warren (Oxford: Oxford University Press, 2018), 113–31.

15. Seyla Benhabib, "Toward a Deliberative Model of Democratic Legitimacy," in *Democracy and Difference: Contesting the Boundaries of the Political*, ed. Seyla Benhabib (Princeton, NJ: Princeton University Press, 1996), 67–94.

16. See chap. 4, as well as Benjamin Braun et al., "Planning Laissez-Faire: Supranational Central Banking and Structural Reforms," *SocArXiv*, March 16, 2021, https://doi.org/10.31235/osf.io/dp3nv.

17. The Parliament is also consulted regarding the appointment of the members of the directory of the ECB. But the decision is made by the European Council (that is, the heads of state or of the government in European states).

18. Deirdre Curtin, "Accountable Independence of the European Central Bank: Seeing the Logics of Transparency," *European Law Journal* 23, no. 1 (2017): 28–44; Adina Akbik, *The European Parliament as an Accountability Forum: Overseeing the Economic and Monetary Union* (Cambridge: Cambridge University Press, 2022).

19. Pervenche Berès, "The European Central Bank: What Accountability to the European Parliament, Corollary of Its Independence in Order to Assure Its Credibility and Its Legitimacy?," *Revue d'économie financière* 144, no. 4 (2021): 227–45.

20. Sebastian Diessner and Stanislas Jourdan, *From Dialogue to Scrutiny: Strengthening the Parliamentary Oversight of the European Central Bank*, Positive Money Europe, 2019; Collectif, "La BCE devrait avoir un mandat politique clair qui expliciterait quels

objectifs secondaires sont les plus pertinents pour l'UE," *Le Monde*, April 9, 2021. It is also essential that the ECB improve its transparency, especially in connection with potential conflicts of interest.

21. James Fishkin, *When the People Speak: Deliberative Democracy and Public Consultation* (Oxford: Oxford University Press, 2011), 160.

22. Benoît Cœuré, "Economics as a Profession: From Science to Practice" (remarks at the Paris School of Economics job forum, November 28, 2019). The US Federal Reserve employed 808 economists in 2017. The exact number of economists in the central banks is not easy to determine because of the institutionally vague definition of that profession. In all, the Eurosystem employed 48,500 persons in 2020.

23. Peter Dietsch, François Claveau, and Clément Fontan, *Do Central Banks Serve the People?* (Cambridge: Polity, 2018).

24. Brian Fabo et al., "Fifty Shades of QE: Conflicts of Interest in Economic Research," NBER Working Paper 27849 (September 2020; revised April 2021).

25. Stéphanie Hennette et al., *How to Democratize Europe* (Cambridge, MA: Harvard University Press, 2019).

26. For a critical presentation of their works and the debates to which they have given rise, see Andreas Follesdal and Andreas Simon Hix, "Why There Is a Democratic Deficit in the EU: A Response to Majone and Moravcsik," *Journal of Common Market Studies* 44, no. 3 (2006): 533–62.

27. Fritz W. Scharpf, *Governing in Europe: Effective and Democratic?* (Oxford: Oxford University Press, 1999).

28. Paul Magnette, *Le régime politique de l'Union européenne* (Paris: Presses de Sciences Po, 2017).

29. For a summary of these criticisms, see Michel Aglietta and Nicolas Leron, *La double démocratie: Une Europe politique pour la croissance* (Paris: Odile Jacob, 2017); Follesdal and Hix, "Why There Is a Democratic Deficit in the EU."

30. Antoine Vauchez, *Democratizing Europe* (New York: Palgrave MacMillan, 2016).

31. Peter Gauweiler and Others v. Deutscher Bundestag, case C-62/15, European Union Court of Justice (grande chambre), ruling of June 16, 2015, § 6.

32. Nik de Boer and Jens van 't Klooster, "The ECB, the Courts and the Issue of Democratic Legitimacy after *Weiss*," *Common Market Law Review* 57, no. 6 (2020).

33. Consolidated Version of the Treaty on European Union, Articles 4, 20, and 40.

34. Leah Downey, "Governing Public Credit Creation," *New Political Economy* 28, no. 1 (2023): 42–56.

35. Lev Menand, *The Fed Unbound: Central Banking in a Time of Crisis* (New York: Columbia Global Reports, 2022); Morgan Ricks, *The Money Problem: Rethinking Financial Regulation* (Chicago: University of Chicago Press, 2016).

36. Peter Conti-Brown and David A. Wishnick, "Technocratic Pragmatism, Bureaucratic Expertise, and the Federal Reserve," *Yale Law Journal* 130 (2020): 546–777 (636).

37. Christina Parajon Skinner, "Central Bank Activism," *Duke Law Journal* 71 (2021): 247–328.

38. Robert C. Hockett and Saule T. Omarova, "Private Wealth and Public Goods: A Case for a National Investment Authority," *Journal of Corporate Law* 43 (2017): 437–91; Saule Omarova, "The National Investment Authority: A Blueprint," Berggruen Institute White Paper, March 23, 2022, https://www.berggruen.org/ideas/articles/the-national -investment-authority-a-blueprint/.

39. William Oman and Romain Svartzman, "What Justifies Sustainable Finance Measures? Financial-Economic Interactions and Possible Implications for Policymakers," *CESifo Forum* 22, no. 3 (2021): 3–11.

40. Philippe Martin, Éric Monnet, and Xavier Ragot, "What Else Can the European Central Bank Do?," *Notes du Conseil d'analyse économique* 5, no. 26 (June 2021): 1–12.

41. Didier Blanchet and Marc Fleurbaey, "De quoi le PIB est la mesure et comment le dépasser," *La vie des idées* (Collège de France), February 2, 2021, https://laviedesidees .fr/IMG/pdf/20210102_pibsoutenable.pdf; Didier Blanchet and Marc Fleurbaey, *Beyond GDP: Measuring Welfare and Assessing Sustainability* (Oxford: Oxford University Press, 2013).

Index

Page numbers in *italics* refer to figures and tables.

modification and, 32–34, 38, 42–43,
140; democratization and, 136, 141,
160–66; digital currencies and, 92–93;
environmental issues and, 164–66;
hyperinflation, 18, 20, 25, 100; interest
rates and, 41, 46, 50–51, 55, 59, 70,
92–96, 113, 136, 160–61; Keynes on,
169n1; monetary policy and, 95; policy
issues and, 2–10, 95–96, 99–101, 106,
113, 120; welfare state and, 18–20,
25–28, 32, 41, 169n1
insurance: central bank function of,
34–38; and creating money, 56, 60;
debt and, 73, 75; democratization and,
141, 151; policy issues and, 96, 109–12,
116, 118, 124; protection and, 1, 3, 6, 12;
welfare state and, 22, 25, 29, 34–43
interbank loans: BIS and, 80, 83; China
and, 81; conditional credit and, 82; debt
and, 79, 81; International Monetary
Fund (IMF) and, 80–82; monetary system and, 80; power and, 78–79; public
debt and, 81; quantitative easing (QE)
and, 79; swap lines, 78–82
interest rates: and creating money, 46,
50–52, 57–59; credit policy and, 121–23,
126; debt and, 64, 67, 70–73, 76, 84–85;
democratization and, 135, 159–61;
digital currencies and, 90–93; engine
of state and, 38–40; external value
and, 111; inflation and, 41, 46, 50–51, 55,
59, 70, 92–96, 113, 136, 160–61; Keynes
on, 95; macroprudential policy and,
113, 115; manipulation of, 95–96; policy
issues and, 95–96, 108, 111, 113, 115,
121–23, 126; protection and, 1, 11; welfare state and, 19, 29, 34, 36, 39–41
International Monetary Fund (IMF):
capital controls and, 176n25; debt

and, 69, 80; financial flows and,
84–85; interbank loans and, 80–82;
liquid assets and, 81; macroprudential
policy and, 120; swap lines and, 80–82
internet, 88
interventions: bonds and, 35; budgetary
policy and, 10; and creating money,
45–46, 59; credit policy and, 126; debt
and, 63–64, 71, 84–85; democratization and, 131, 153, 159, 167–68; external
value and, 112; Polanyi and, 6, 32–33,
38, 80; policy issues and, 96, 112, 114,
119–26, 129; protection and, 3, 6, 10–12;
state, 10, 29, 59, 84, 114, 168; welfare
state and, 19, 26–35, 37, 39
investing: bonds, 35–36, 41, 52, 68, 77, 101,
124, 161; and creating money, 53–54, 57,
59; credit policy and, 122, 125, 127–29;
debt and, 70, 72, 74, 86; democratization and, 141, 143, 147, 149, 153–61, 164,
168; digital currencies and, 94; external value and, 111–12; macroprudential
policy and, 118; protection and, 6–7,
12, 14; shareholders, 5, 27, 55–57, 127,
173n11; stocks, 52–53, 106, 111; welfare
state and, 24, 36–37, 40–43
investment banks: central banks and,
40–42; and creating money, 59; credit
policy and, 122, 127–28; debt and, 72;
democratization and, 141, 147, 149, 157,
159, 168; digital currencies and, 94;
European, 41; French, 41; protection
and, 7; vs. central banks, 40–42
Iran, 83
Italy, 27, 102

Japan, 171n13; and creating money, 52;
credit policy and, 123, 126; debt and,
65, *66*, 70, 75–79; democratization

monetary policy (*continued*)
and, 6–11, 14–15; as public good, 17–23; sovereignty and, 98, 102, 104; stability and, 6, 10–11, 31, 43, 61, 71, 79, 84, 86–87, 98, 102, 104, 111, 113, 117–21, 129, 135, 141, 144–45, 163, 166; welfare state and, 17–23, 29, 31, 33, 41, 43, 172n26
money market funds, 119, 179n31
money multiplier, 49
moral hazard, 35, 69, 171n24
Moravcsik, Andrew, 150–52
mortgage-backed securities (MBSs), 127
mortgage markets, 35, 42, 79, 127

National Investment Authority (NIA), 157
Nazism, 30, 101
neoliberalism, 29
Network of Central Banks and Supervisors for Greening the Financial System (NGFS), 97
New Deal, 27–28, 157
New Zealand, 99
Nixon, Richard, 100
Norman, Montagu, 169n2

Obama, Barack, 102
Office of Inspector General (OIG), 155
online purchases, 86, 89
outright monetary transactions (OMT), 69–70
overdrafts, 67

pandemic emergency purchase programme (PEPP), 65
paper money, 29, 90
pensions, 32, 51, 54
People's Bank of China, 81, 90–91, 97, 100, 177n8
Piketty, Thomas, 51

Poland, 80
Polanyi, Karl, 6, 32–33, 38, 80
policy issues: Bank of England and, 103; central bank systems and, 105–9; centralization, 27–28, 60, 179n28; China and, 97–98, 120, 125; commercial banks and, 106–8, 123–24; confidence in currency and, 109–10; coordination and, 102, 116, 119; COVID-19 pandemic and, 2, 10–11, 97, 119, 125, 180nn41–42; credit, 121–29; debt and, 96, 101–3, 106, 108–12, 117–18, 123–26, 177n10, 179n38; decentralization, 60, 88, 107, 109, 143; decision-making and, 105–7, 113, 118; decommodification, 32–34, 38, 42–43, 140; democratic control and, 2–9, 13–14, 97–98, 105–6, 122, 126, 129; deposits and, 108–9, 120, 122; ecological transition and, 119, 128; environmental issues and, 112, 126; European Central Bank (ECB) and, 101–9, 115–16, 121, 123, 128, 177n10, 179n28; eurozone and, 177n5; exchange rate and, 95–96, 98, 109–12; external value of currency and, 109–13; Federal Reserve System and, 105–7, 109, 116; financial crisis of 2008 and, 96, 115–19, 124, 127–28; Financial Policy Committee and, 118; France and, 101, 108; independence and, 97–107, 115, 117, 126, 129; inequality and, 122; inflation and, 2–10, 95–96, 99–101, 106, 113, 120; insurance, 96, 109–12, 116, 118, 124; interest rates, 95–96, 108, 111, 113, 115, 121–23, 126; interventions, 96, 112, 114, 119–26, 129; legal, 98–107, 116, 124–25, 129–38, 148, 153, 156–57; legitimacy and, 97, 101, 106–7, 118, 120, 122, 129; lender of last resort and, 116, 124; liberalism and, 4,

democratization and, 132, 141, 145, 150, 153, 156–59, 164; digital currencies and, 91; European Systemic Risk Board, 118; hazards, 3, 26, 35, 69, 112, 171n24; policy issues and, 103, 109, 112–19, 129, 179n33; protection and, 5–6; reinjecting, 52–54; welfare state and, 18, 31, 35, 39, 43, 171n24

Roosevelt, Franklin D., 27

Rosanvallon, Pierre, 135, 138, 152

salaries, 18–20, 50, 89, 92, 102

sanctions, 83

savings: and creating money, 50–51, 54; debt and, 176n30; digital currencies and, 87, 94; welfare state and, 20, 170n3

scandal, 29

Scharpf, Fritz, 150

schemes, 54, 72

securities: and creating money, 45–49, 54–55; credit policy and, 121–23, 127; debt and, 63–64, 68, 72, 76, 82; democratization and, 161; digital currencies and, 89; external value and, 111; mortgage-backed, 127; protection and, 11; welfare state and, 35, 37

shadow banks, 22, 28, 53, 154

shareholders, 5, 27, 55–57, 127, 173n11

shocks, 38, 160

silver, 173n2

Skinner, Christina Parajon, 156

social welfare, 6, 73

sovereignty: Bank of England and, 103; bonds and, 101; cross-country perspective on, 98–105; economists and, 100, 103; European Union (EU) and, 101; eurozone and, 99, 102; guarantees and, 98, 104; indepen-

dence and, 98–105; Japan and, 102; legal issues and, 98–105; monetary policy and, 98, 102, 104; policy issues and, 98–105; public service and, 102; quantitative easing (QE) and, 102–3; regulations and, 98–100; stability and, 99; taxes and, 102; United Kingdom and, 102–3

Spain, 108, 118

special interests, 1, 59

special-purpose vehicle, 125

speculation: bankruptcy and, 30; and creating money, 53, 58–59; digital currencies and, 88; liquidity and, 42, 172n35; welfare state and, 37, 43

stability: and creating money, 58–61; debt and, 64–65, 68–69, 71, 79–80, 84–85; democratization and, 131, 134–35, 140–41, 144–45, 148, 151, 153, 158–59, 163–66; digital currencies and, 86–88, 91; Dornbusch on, 134; European Stability Mechanism (ESM) and, 69–70, 151; as explicit objective, 60–61; Financial Stability Oversight Council (FSOC) and, 118–19; governing statutes for, 99; microeconomic policy and, 114; monetary policy and, 6, 10–11, 31, 43, 61, 71, 79, 84–87, 98, 102–4, 111–13, 117–21, 129, 135, 141, 144–45, 163, 166; policy issues and, 96–99, 102, 104, 111–14, 117–21, 124, 127, 129; protection and, 4–11; public good and, 17–23; sovereignty and, 99; welfare state and, 17–25, 28, 31, 33, 37, 39, 42–43

stablecoins, 89

standing facilities, 35, 124, 172n26

Stiglitz, Joseph, 132–33, 136, 138

stocks, 52–53, 106, 111

US Congress: central bank systems and,
105–7; debt and, 73, 82; democratization and, 147, 154–57; digital currencies and, 91; policy issues and, 102,
105–7, 117, 125; protection and, 8

value of money, 6, 43, 160
Vauchez, Antoine, 151
Venezuela, 83

wages, 10, 25, 51, 153
welfare state: Bank of England and, 24,
40, 172n26; budgetary policy and,
42; central bank systems and, 25–32;
China and, 33, 42, 172n34; commercial
banks and, 21–22, 35, 170n7, 171n24;
confidence in currency and, 17–21,
28; coordination and, 20; COVID-19
pandemic and, 26, 29; credit policy
and, 28, 42; debt and, 20, 23–32, 35, 37,
39–42; decommodification and, 32–34,
38, 42–43, 140; democracy and, 75, 142,
167; democratic control and, 17, 38, 43;
deposits and, 21–24, 41, 170n3, 170n7;
distinctions and, 37; ecological transition and, 41–44; economists and, 29,
34, 37; environmental issues and, 43;
European Central Bank (ECB) and,
26, 31, 35, 42–43, 171n20; European
debt crisis and, 69; exchange rate and,
19, 169n2; Federal Reserve System and,
27, 32, 40; financial crises and, 18, 20,
22, 26, 29–34, 38–39, 170n7; financing,
3; France and, 27, 41, 170; government
debt and, 23–32; Great Depression
and, 20, 25–26, 28, 30; growth and, 27;
guarantees and, 17, 21, 24, 35–41, 92,
173n1; independence and, 23, 26–27,
31–33, 42, 169n2; inflation and, 18–20,
25–28, 32, 41, 169n1; insurance and, 22,

25, 29, 34–43; interest rates and, 19, 29,
34, 36, 39–41; interventions and, 19, 26,
27–35, 37, 39; investing and, 24, 36–37,
40–43; legal issues and, 32, 169n2,
171n20; legitimacy and, 17, 26, 28; lender
of last resort and, 35; liberalism and,
22, 24, 28–39, 171n18; liquidity and, 24,
33–40, 43, 171n24, 172n35; loans and,
24, 34–41, 170n3; loss of confidence in
currency and, 19–20; macroeconomic
policies and, 20, 27–30, 43; markets
and, 18, 22–25, 28–43; monetary
policy and, 17–23, 29, 31, 33, 41, 43,
172n26; policy issues and, 96–97;
power and, 18, 28–29, 36, 40; prices
and, 18–20, 169n1; principles of, 4;
private banks and, 22, 26–28, 41; protection and, 3–6, 14–15; public development banks and, 40; public good
and, 17–23; public service and, 22,
33; real estate and, 18, 35, 41; reform
and, 27; regulations and, 20, 22, 31,
33–34, 39, 41–43; risk and, 18, 31, 35,
39, 43, 171n24; savings and, 20, 170n3;
securities and, 35, 37; speculation and,
37, 43; stability and, 17–25, 28, 31, 33,
37, 39, 42–43; Treasury and, 24, 40, 42;
uncertainty and, 18; unemployment
and, 20, 26, 30; United Kingdom and,
35; United States and, 27–32, 35–36,
40, 42, 170n5, 170n9; World War II era
and, 24–26, 28, 30, 32

Werner plan, 121
Wishnick, David A., 155–56
World War I era, 40, 96, 174n13
World War II era: debt and, 72–73, 82;
democratization and, 147; policy
issues and, 104, 114; protection and,
3, 5; welfare state and, 24–26, 28,
30, 32